Your exclusive ticket to

a Gooseberry Patch adventure!

When a new season is drawing near, there's nothing more exciting than pulling out favorite recipes and getting inspired. As an **exclusive, free gift** for Gooseberry Patch email subscribers, Vickie and JoAnn are creating **limited edition collections** of the very best of the seasons.

These handcrafted seasonal guides (**$9.95 value**) are full of our favorite recipes, inspiring photos, DIY tips and holiday ideas – you'll be celebrating all season long! A new issue will be released 4 times per year and each one is available for a limited time only.

If you haven't signed up yet, come aboard. Your subscription is your ticket to year 'round inspiration – and it's completely free!

www.gooseberrypatch.com/signup

Visit our website today, add your name to our email list, and you'll be able to download our latest seasonal preview instantly!

Find Gooseberry Patch
wherever you are!

www.gooseberrypatch.com

Call us toll-free at 1·800·854·6673

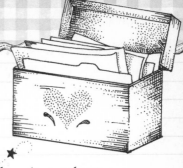

YOUR recipe could appear in our next cookbook!

Share your tried & true family favorites with us instantly at
www.gooseberrypatch.com

If you'd rather jot 'em down by hand, just mail this form to...
Gooseberry Patch • Cookbooks – Call for Recipes
2545 Farmers Dr., #380 • Columbus, OH 43235

If your recipe is selected for a book, you'll receive a FREE copy!

Please share only your original recipes or those that you have made your own over the years.

Recipe Name:

Number of Servings:

Any fond memories about this recipe? Special touches you like to add
or handy shortcuts?

Ingredients (include specific measurements):

Instructions (continue on back if needed):

Special Code: **cookbookspage**

Over ➤

Extra space for recipe if needed:

Tell us about yourself...

Your complete contact information is needed so that we can send you your FREE cookbook, if your recipe is published. Phone numbers and email addresses are kept private and will only be used if we have questions about your recipe.

Name:

Address:

City: State: Zip:

Email:

Daytime Phone:

Thank you! Vickie & Jo Ann

Gooseberry Patch
2545 Farmers Dr., #380
Columbus, OH 43235

www.gooseberrypatch.com
1•800•854•6673

Copyright 2014, Gooseberry Patch 978-1-62093-170-7
Second Printing, July, 2014

This edition contains the same content as *Slow-Cooker
Christmas Favorites* (ISBN 978-1-62093-138-7).

U.S. to Metric Recipe Equivalents

Volume Measurements

1/4 teaspoon	1 mL
1/2 teaspoon	2 mL
1 teaspoon	5 mL
1 tablespoon = 3 teaspoons	15 mL
2 tablespoons = 1 fluid ounce	30 mL
1/4 cup	60 mL
1/3 cup	75 mL
1/2 cup = 4 fluid ounces	125 mL
1 cup = 8 fluid ounces	250 mL
2 cups = 1 pint =16 fluid ounces	500 mL
4 cups = 1 quart	1 L

Weights

1 ounce	30 g
4 ounces	120 g
8 ounces	225 g
16 ounces = 1 pound	450 g

Oven Temperatures

300° F	150° C
325° F	160° C
350° F	180° C
375° F	190° C
400° F	200° C
450° F	230° C

Baking Pan Sizes

Square

8x8x2 inches	2 L = 20x20x5 cm
9x9x2 inches	2.5 L = 23x23x5 cm

Rectangular

13x9x2 inches	3.5 L = 33x23x5 cm

Loaf

9x5x3 inches	2 L = 23x13x7 cm

Round

8x1-1/2 inches	1.2 L = 20x4 cm
9x1-1/2 inches	1.5 L = 23x4 cm

Contents

Dedication

To everyone who still loves making snowmen, mugs of hot cocoa and peeking under the Christmas tree.

Appreciation

Our heartiest thanks to the terrific cooks who shared their best slow-cooker recipes...happy holidays to you!

The Magic of
Christmas

Christmas Day

Jessica Delia
McGraw, NY

My father was one of sixteen children. Every Christmas, my parents and siblings would drive to Grandma's house for dinner. At least fifty of my aunts, uncles and cousins would be there. The decorated Christmas tree was always perfect, with gifts for everyone underneath. The house would be filled with the delicious smells of the holiday... homemade pies and fruit breads, roast turkey, baked ham, potatoes, squash, pickles, all homegrown and made with love by my grandma. Everyone was happy, loving and laughing, having such a good time together. We never left hungry! My father has since passed on, but Grandma is still baking and making things from scratch. And we still gather as often as we can.

At holiday dinners, use a special tablecloth and ask family members, friends and special visitors to sign it with fabric markers. Sure to become a cherished tradition!

The Magic of Christmas

Baking with Grandma

Stephani Hatmaker
West Union, OH

Every year my grandma and I always baked cookies, pies and cakes together. Our special time together was in the kitchen, and at Christmas it was so much more fun. We made all kinds of cookies, pies and cakes. With Christmas music playing in the background, we always made a big mess, with flour and sugar everywhere like fallen snow. I loved watching her cook. I remember saying, "Grandma, I will never be able to cook as good as you." And she always said, "Sis, you're my grandkid, I know you will be a good cook." Well, Grandma is gone now, but her old cookbooks and love of cooking never died...those she passed down to me. What fine memories I have of Grandma and me in her kitchen. Each Christmas I smile and think to myself, I bet those angels in heaven love her peanut butter pies!

Dig into Mom's or Grandma's recipe box for that extra-special dessert you remember...and then bake some to share with the whole family.

Christmas at Star Lake

Heather Ingraham
Barrie, Ontario

When I was a child, my grandparents owned Star Lake Lodge near Rosseau, Ontario. Every Christmas Eve, they would keep the store open late and invite everyone they knew to stop by! Santa would arrive sitting on the tailgate of a pick-up truck, with a sack of gifts for all of us kids. Games were set up for the kids too. Everyone would crowd into the diner part of the store to eat pie with ice cream, drink hot chocolate and sing Christmas carols. Those were the best years and memories of my life!

Blizzard of '49

Karen Overholt
Kennewick, WA

It was the winter of 1949. To our delight, we had a blizzard and more snow than we knew what to do with. It didn't take long for the kids on Alder Street to team up and build igloos, which were well stocked with snowballs. Before we could say "Get ready, set, go!" our folks came out ready to do battle on each side of the street and what a time they had. We kids stood back and watched in disbelief. My father is gone now, as are most of those that were there that day. But that memory is 64 years old and it still warms my heart.

Craft a fun snowball wreath that won't melt! Hot-glue fuzzy white pompoms over a foam wreath, then top it with a simple bow.

The Magic of Christmas

Country Christmas Tree

Anita Green
Clarendon, AR

When I was young, I remember trudging into the woods with my older brother to find that perfect Christmas tree. We would drag the tree home with frosty fingers and red noses, but with so much excitement. Once Daddy evened up the cut and put it on a tree stand we were ready. Out came the paper for making paper chains, as well as old ornaments that probably should have been thrown away years ago, but to us they were bright and shiny and meant Christmas. We always put on tons of icicles, really too many, but hey, it was Christmas! Presents were few, but the tree was the main event, along with Mom's wonderful holiday meal, cookies, pies and cakes. Those were indeed the best times.

A deep shadow box is a perfect way to enjoy fragile vintage ornaments.
Line the inside of the box with gift wrap or cut-outs from Christmas cards.

Best Christmas Ever

Tamra Pierce
Carriere, MS

When I was a sophomore in high school, my family had a fire in our house just before Thanksgiving. Having to spend Thanksgiving in a hotel and not getting back into our house until two or three days before Christmas, we knew we were not going to get many gifts that year. We were just thankful that we were all safe and back in our own home. On Christmas Eve, there was a knock on the door. When we answered the door, no one was there...but a big box of gifts had been left on the porch. The Lord had sent someone (maybe Santa!) to bring us gifts of clothes and toys. Thankful for someone's generosity, we began to cry with happiness. That year my family truly knew the full meaning of Christmas and the wonderful effect that giving can have on others.

When you go out on Christmas Eve to attend church services or see the Christmas lights, share a plate of homemade cookies with your local fire house or police station...such a neighborly gesture.

The Magic of Christmas

Dad as Santa

Karen Mullins
Creston, OH

I'm the oldest of eight children. I don't know how my parents did it, but we always had a great Christmas. Christmas Eve has always been celebrated at our house with a huge party that included close and extended family & friends. Anyone who wanted to join the festivities was welcome. Around 9 pm on Christmas Eve, we'd hear a knock on the door...lo and behold, there stood Santa with a big red bag of gifts for all the children, and a few for the adults too. Boy oh boy, were we kids special to have Santa stop at our house on the one night that we knew he was extra busy! We must have been extra good that year. Not only did Dad play Santa every year for us, but many years he did it for all the kids in our town. He rode in our town's Christmas parade, waving and calling out to many of the children by name, and then would sit in the gazebo downtown (rain, snow or shine) until everyone got to sit on his lap and give him their lists. Dad continued to play Santa until a year before he passed away in 1993. My brother has now taken over the Santa duties at our yearly family celebration and his ho-ho-ho is nearly as good as the one we heard for all those years!

When you have family members visiting for the holidays, be sure to get out the old picture albums, slides and family films. What a joy to reminisce together, laugh and share special memories of childhood and Christmases past!

Moving During a Snowstorm...Yikes!
Christine Camaj
North Salem, NY

In 1994, my boys Robert and Antonino were seven and eight. We moved from the city to a quiet rural town in upstate New York during one of the worst snowstorms we have seen! Though it was hectic living out of boxes those first few days, the snow was glistening laid out in our big new backyard. The boys were having a blast and at one point, amongst the huge drifts on the sides of the house and trees, I could not find them. All I could see was their hats on top of their little heads and their little hands waving at me to come and play! We had never before seen so much snow. Now we play outside with my 4-year-old granddaughter Jolie and though we've had some heavy snowstorms it is still nothing like it was in 1994. We've never forgotten it, and twenty years later I am proud to say my little snowmen are now a fireman and a doctor! It's my fondest memory of my little big guys playing in the wintertime.

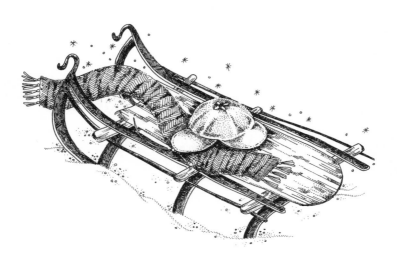

Throw an impromptu sledding party for the first snowfall! Gather friends & neighbors to enjoy some snow fun and then head back home for a cozy fire and mugs of hot cocoa or mulled cider.

The Magic of Christmas

Christmas Blizzard of 1947

Arden Regnier
East Moriches, NY

Christmas Day for a seven-year-old was such a joy. Santa filled my stocking to the top and I found lots of presents under the tree too. Grandma had baked hundreds of cookies the week before and we had a big family Christmas dinner with more presents. What more could a kid want? That evening during the wee hours of the morning it began to snow, dropping over two feet of snow on Long Island, New York. It was the blizzard of 1947 crippling New York City. In a time before snow throwers or electric shovels, my dad was out there shoveling the driveway and a path to our front door. The snowplows came through and the driveway was buried again, bringing the snow well over my head. What a fun time I had building snow forts with our friends, having snowball fights, sleigh riding and climbing the mountain the snowplow left in front of our house. I'm not sure what was more fun, the excitement of Christmas with all its gifts, goodies and family time, or days of playing in the snow.

A winter snow kit for the car is a gift any driver would appreciate. Pack a duffle bag with a snow scraper, a warm pair of new gloves, a folding snow shovel and a flashlight. Tie on a big tag that says, "Thinking warm thoughts of you!"

A Magical Childhood Christmas

Marilyn Gasaway
Louisville, KY

Growing up in the '40s and '50s was a magical time, especially at Christmas. About a week before Christmas, my dad, two brothers and I would pick out a real tree to bring home. It was such fun getting out the ornaments and decorating the tree...wonderful cut-glass ornaments, handmade ornaments and even some of the whimsical type. Our tree was the most beautiful thing I had ever seen. As Christmas neared, there was much to do...cleaning, baking cookies and cakes and wrapping all the presents for relatives. On Christmas Eve we would start getting ready for the festivities right after supper. Santa always made his way to our house during this time. We could hear his ho-ho-ho's, questions if we were good little boys and girls, and the jingle bells of the reindeer. Joey, Don and I would run into the living room, so excited, but we always just missed Santa. A new baby doll, a toy train, coloring books and other gifts filled the room. It wasn't long before the house was alive with music and laughter as aunts, uncles, cousins and grandparents arrived. I really loved sharing the holidays with family. Later that night we would all attend the midnight Christmas Eve candlelight service at church. It was a perfect way to end a magical day. Growing up, we didn't have much in the way of money but we had a wealth of love and joy of family...the simple things we remember for a lifetime. I will strive to maintain these old-fashioned Christmases for my grandchildren.

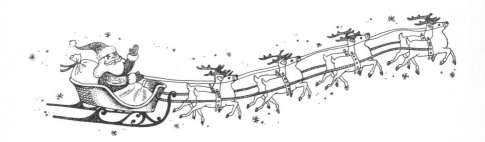

Set up a small tree in the kids' rooms...a great way for them to show off homemade and favorite ornaments of their very own.

The Magic of Christmas

Mom's Backroom Goodies

Ruthann Houle
Massena, NY

My special Christmas memory is of my mother's backroom, as she called it. It was an extra room on our home and did not have a basement under it. As we lived in upstate New York, that room was very cold in the wintertime. Every year in November, Mother started baking her Christmas goodies and storing them in the backroom. She made candy, cookies, breads, even fruitcake...and everyone liked her fruitcake! She would make gift baskets for so many loved ones and friends. As it got closer to Christmas the room would get fuller of these great treats. I remember every time the door to the backroom opened, the best aroma of all the goodies came rushing out. It was wonderful! I'll never forget the delicious smell and all the love that went into her baking and filling that backroom.

Christmas Magic

Karen Seagraves
London, OH

One year when my boys were very little, about three and five, "Santa" completely forgot to fill their Christmas stockings. I was in the kitchen making the usual huge Christmas morning breakfast. My sister, who lived with me, managed to sneak the stockings into the kitchen, where I filled them, then we sneaked them back to the fireplace mantle. About thirty minutes later I heard a commotion in the living room and the screeching of two little boys hollering, "It's magic, Mom, it's magic!" Santa had come back and filled the stockings.

Watch tag sales for good-as-new Christmas tins, canning jars and other containers to fill with holiday goodies. Dress up jar lids with a pinked circle of homespun...tins just need a liner of parchment paper.

Daddy's Candle

Karen McLendon
Pensacola, FL

Many years ago, when I was about six, my father decided we would make my mother a special Christmas present. He had found a cone-shaped orange juice container and thought it would make a nice candle. He made the candle and let it harden, then drizzled wax down the sides while we watched, for hours it seemed. I am not sure what my mother thought of the candle at the time, but every year that candle still burns at our Christmas...at least for a short time, because it has to last awhile yet. The candle is now 48 years old. We lost my father years ago, so this Christmas memory is very sweet to me.

The Christmas Bow

Lyn Levasseur
Salisbury, MA

When my Mémère was living, she placed a special Christmas bow on my very first Christmas present. From that day forward that bow was kept and placed on one family member's Christmas gift year after year. Every other bow was tossed out, but not the big red bow. Whoever got that bow was thrilled, because it was something special. Even after Mémère passed away, the bow continued to make its rounds. I'm sorry to say that after 48 Christmases the Christmas bow fell apart and we had to put it to rest, but it's such a wonderful memory of my grandmother and her little Christmas tradition.

Start a sweet new tradition at your holiday dinner...hand out paper star cut-outs and have each person write down what they're happiest for since last Christmas.

The Magic of Christmas

Christmas Eve Scavenger Hunt

Chris Scrivo
Venetia, PA

I am the mother of three boys, Nathan, Andrew and Aaron. When they were little it was always difficult to get them dressed and out the door to church on Christmas Eve, so we began a tradition of having birthday cake for Jesus after church. Also, I collect nativity sets and never put the babies in the mangers until Christmas Eve. So we decided that as the boys grew, and my collection grew too, that it was quite fun to match each baby with the set he went with. When we would all head out to church, my dining room table was already set with the birthday cake and a platter with all the Baby Jesus figures on it. We would return home, light the advent candles, sing "Happy Birthday," then place each baby in the manger. Now in their twenties, my boys still comment when they see a nativity set complete with a baby displayed before Christmas Eve. Special times together!

Patchwork Christmas stockings are a sweet way to share a cherished old quilt that's become very worn. Cut simple stocking shapes from the best portions of the quilt, stitch together and trim with tea-dyed lace.

Santa's Secret Codes

Jamie Cabral
Meridian, ID

When I was growing up, there were four kids in our family, with my sisters Jennifer and LuAnn, my brother Tom and me being the youngest. On Christmas morning, we were not allowed to go down the hall to the living room until Dad had checked to see if Santa had come. If we got up too early, he told us we had to go back to bed! I guess that was how he and my mom were able to sleep in for a few more minutes on Christmas. Then, when he announced that Santa had indeed arrived, we would go into the living room and see the beautiful tree and all of the presents, but wait! Santa had put a special code on the gifts and only my dad had the answers! So this way, Dad controlled the opening of the gifts and it made Christmas morning last longer. One time "Santa" made a mistake and I opened up my brother's underwear! As an extra treat, Mom let us kids eat Christmas cookies for breakfast, just on this one special day. The gift codes are a tradition that I have continued with my own children and it is so much fun to see the excitement of the others getting to watch their siblings open their gifts.

Make time for your town's special holiday events. Whether it's a Christmas parade, Santa arriving by horse-drawn sleigh or a tree lighting ceremony, hometown traditions make the best memories!

The Magic of Christmas

Christmas Angel

Gretta DeMennato
Bel Air, MD

The Christmas that I was eleven years old, my parents had separated in September. It had been a long time coming. My mom was amazing. She skipped meals, did without things herself and made every effort to save money for Christmas. I was aware of our money struggles but, thankfully my brother Steve, seven years old, was not. I mentioned in a letter to my Uncle Pat, whom Mom had raised, that things were tough and I wanted Steve to still believe in Santa. At Thanksgiving, Uncle Pat surprised us with a visit home from the Army. He told me not to worry about the money and that Steve would still remember Santa. When my mom arrived home from taking him back to the airport, she was in tears. Mom told me that Uncle Pat had given his entire month's pay to her so that we could have a good Christmas. It was the best Christmas ever, because we knew the best gift was family!

Keep the Christmas dinner menu simple, familiar and yummy. You may even want to ask your family ahead of time what dishes are special to them. It's a day for tradition and comfort...and you'll be more relaxed too.

An Extended Family Christmas Celebration

Judy Loemker
Edwardsville, IL

We are so very blessed each Christmas to get together with our
extended family...aunts and uncles, cousins, second cousins, third
cousins and spouses. The Steinmann clan, well over 140 people now,
still meets the day after Christmas for our annual family gathering,
even though our dear grandparents, Walter and Bertha, passed away
about thirty years ago. Grandpa and Grandma were fortunate to have
eight wonderful children who gave them so many offspring. They
would have loved to see how their family has grown! This event runs
like clockwork. Each year, two families are responsible for party
planning. They rent a hall or use a church basement, now that our
group has grown too large to fit into one of our aunt's homes. A pretty
Christmas tree and other decorations are put up, everyone brings
delicious food and the little ones draw names ahead of time and bring
gifts to exchange that night. Games are played, both by children and
adults, the delicious food is served, and great conversations abound.
But the very best part of our evening comes when the candles are lit,
the lights are turned out, and we all join in singing familiar Christmas
carols together, most in English, but a few sung in German. Many of
the aunts and uncles still harmonize to the carols. It sometimes brings
tears to our eyes as we enjoy the beautiful music and remember those
who are no longer with us. The greatest joy we have, though, is being
together and celebrating the true meaning of Christmas...that of our
Savior's birth! This amazing tradition has been in our family for over
sixty years now. As I said before, we are truly blessed!

The perfect Christmas tree?
All Christmas trees are perfect!

– Charles N. Barnard

The Magic of Christmas

Christmas Eve Walks

Barbara Cissell
Louisville, KY

Every Christmas Eve, no matter how cold it was outside, my dad would bundle up my siblings Margi, Kenny, Betty and me. Then he took us out for a walk around the neighborhood so we could look for the Christmas star. We never did find it, but enjoyed looking at all the Christmas lights, because we knew that while we were out, "Santa" would come and place all our gifts around the tree. That was an exciting and very magic time. The funny thing was, Mom never came along on any of those walks with us!

Christmas Dinner Table Gifts

Helen D'Amato
Seabrook, NH

For many years now, our family's holiday tradition is to place a miniature sleigh on the Christmas dinner table. It's filled with inexpensive one or two-dollar wrapped gifts, each with a long ribbon and a name tag attached. Before we sit down for dinner we find our own name tag and stand by it. When we all have our ribbons, we count to three and pull a gift from the sleigh. It is a lot of fun. I started this when my children were young. My children are grown now and they have carried on the tradition with their own children. I have told many people about this tradition...they have tried it and love it too.

Fresh red roses or carnations make a delightfully different winter centerpiece. Arrange flowers in a big vase with glossy green holly or delicate ferns.

Meeting Santa

Lisa Merritt
Farmville, VA

At Christmas when I was nine, my mother dressed my three sisters, my brother and me in our Sunday best and we went to Miller & Rhoads department store to see Santa. My father had died just over a year before, so even going to see Santa didn't seem very exciting. The legendary Santa decorations were magical. There was snow, icicles, polar bears and elves, who talked to us while we were waiting to see Santa. Santa was amazing. He was jolly and plump with a long gray beard and hair, wearing a red suit. One of the elves helped my younger siblings to visit with Santa, one at a time. When it was my turn, Santa looked at me, smiled and said,"Hello, Lisa. You've been a very good girl this year." My mouth fell open. He knew my name! He went on, "I know it has been a hard year for you and you deserve something special." He winked. I hugged him and cried. I'm crying now. I don't know how Santa knew, but I really needed him to help me feel like a little girl again and that day he did.

Help your children share the giving spirit of Christmas. Before the holidays, go through their toys with them, pulling out two or three they no longer play with. Clean up the toys and donate them to a shelter or community project for less fortunate children.

The Magic of Christmas

Christmas Can Be Magical

Lois Tanner
American Fork, UT

One Christmas Eve in the late '50s I overheard my grandmother talking. She asked my mother if the doll that my little sister Paula was getting for Christmas had any extra clothes. My mother answered no, that the doll would have only the clothes she came with. I was saddened by that, because I knew how much Paula enjoyed playing with dolls and changing their outfits. I even wondered why Santa wouldn't be bringing her any extra clothes for the doll...and how did Mom even know that my sister was getting a doll from Santa Claus? When it was time to go to bed that night, I still felt a little sad about the conversation I'd overheard, but was so excited about Santa coming that night. I noticed that Grandma had disappeared and I just figured she had gone to bed too. The next morning, not only did the little doll for my sister have a complete extra outfit, including a gown, a diaper, a bonnet and even a blanket, but they were all hand-crocheted from some very familiar yarn that I had seen in Grandma's basket. Grandma had taught me to crochet, so I was pretty quick to figure things out. Grandma seemed to be a little more tired than usual that day, but I noticed that the smiles on Paula's face made Grandma smile too. I will never forget the day that Grandma became a big part of the magic of Christmas.

Host a tree-trimming party. Invite all the cousins, aunts and uncles for a merry time hanging ornaments and twining garland...even set up a table of craft materials so guests can make their own. Afterwards, share holiday plans over a simple supper. Such fun!

Fun, Laughter and Love

Mandy Whalen
Pensacola, FL

Our family's Christmases have not always been like most families' are. When they were small, my children were sometimes awakened in the early morning hours to celebrate with their father and me. He was an airline pilot and commuted to work from North Carolina to Washington, DC, so we would have Santa and then he would leave on his commute. The children would celebrate Christmas Eve with his parents and relatives, then on Christmas Day, once again we would pile in the car and be off to my parents, a wonderful lunch with them and an afternoon with my cousins, their family & friends. When my children share their memories of their childhood Christmas, they always recall how much they loved those days. Our family was always about fun, laughter and love.

I Still Believe in the Jolly Man

Thomas Campbell
Eden Prairie, MN

My favorite memories during the holidays are of family members playing the part of Old Saint Nick. As each child gets old enough, about 16, each gets a chance to be the Jolly Fat Man. I guess I can say I was rather blessed for being a big kid, so I got to play Santa a few times more than others. I would even buy a fake beard and fake glasses to try to fool other people, especially the small ones. It is always fun seeing the smiles of children when Santa is around. Shhh...I still believe in Jolly Old Saint Nick, I just love to play him on Christmas!

If you have a windowbox, spruce it up for winter too. Filled with pine, berries, oranges, apples, nuts and a cranberry garland, it makes a lovely wintertime welcome.

The Magic of Christmas

Christmas Eve Feast

Candy Foltz
Hagerstown, MD

My parents have always made Christmas very special. They would invite many relatives in for a Christmas Eve feast. There would be a fire in the fireplace along with marshmallows for roasting. My father played guitar and would always play Christmas songs for us. We would sing and enjoy each other's company. The evening would end with two stories, Clement C. Moore's "The Night Before Christmas" and the story of Jesus's birth. I loved hearing my Dad read those stories over the years. How awesome it is to have a loving family to share special holidays with.

Family is More Important than Things *Miranda Ching*
Aiea, HI

When I was about eight years old, my mother bought some beautiful bell-shaped blue glass ornaments. She commented often about how much she liked them. As I helped to undress the tree after Christmas, you guessed it, I dropped one of those ornaments and it shattered. I began to cry because I knew how much she loved those bells! She put her arm around me and said, "Honey, it's okay...it's just an ornament." That was one of many instances when she taught me that family is more important than things.

Set up a giftwrap station for carefree wrapping. Gather pretty paper, stickers, gift bags and tissue along with scissors, tape and a pen. Just for fun, make a sign for the door that reads, "Please Knock...Elves at Work!"

The Christmas Bike

Ronda Hauss
Louisville, KY

When our daughter Krista was ten years old, all she wanted for Christmas was a mountain bike. The last gift she opened on Christmas morning was a small box with a note in it. The note contained a riddle she had to solve in order to figure out where the next present was hidden. More riddles took her to the meat drawer of the refrigerator, outside to the clubhouse (where she was certain that the new bike was hidden...she was wrong!), back under the Christmas tree and finally to the bathroom shower. As Krista walked into the bathroom, she exclaimed, "Where is the next present going to send me?" I'll never forget the look on her face when she pulled back the shower curtain. There, stuffed sideways into the shower, was her brand new mountain bike. She was so excited that she stood there jumping up and down begging her daddy to help her get the bike out of the shower so she could ride it. Krista still tells the story of the bike in the shower and she is 28 years old now!

Be sure to share your own family tales at Christmastime...they're super conversation starters. How about the time Grandma set out cookies to cool and her puppy dog ate them, or the year a big snowstorm led to a houseful of extra Christmas guests...it's such fun to share stories like these!

Brunch
Open House

Christmas Breakfast Casserole

Sharon Beaty
Cookeville, TN

*We have eight children and this recipe is one of the main
highlights for all of us on Christmas morning! I love that
it can cook overnight while we're waiting for Santa.*

26-oz. pkg. frozen diced
   potatoes
16-oz. pkg. ground pork
   breakfast sausage
1 doz. eggs

1 c. milk
salt and pepper to taste
16-oz. pkg. shredded Cheddar
   cheese

Spread potatoes in a slow cooker sprayed with non-stick vegetable
spray. Brown sausage in a skillet over medium heat; drain and spread
over potatoes. Beat eggs in a large bowl; whisk in milk, salt and pepper.
Pour egg mixture over sausage. Top with cheese. Cover and cook on
low setting for 6 to 8 hours, until eggs are set. Makes 8 servings.

Put a slow cooker to work on the buffet...set on low, it can keep
sausage gravy, scrambled eggs or other breakfast foods
piping-hot and delicious.

Brunch Open House

Pull-Apart Monkey Bread

Tori Willis
Champaign, IL

My kids love this sweet treat! They like to help too. I put the cinnamon-sugar and biscuits in a plastic zipping bag and let 'em shake the bag until the biscuits are all coated.

3/4 c. sugar
3/4 c. brown sugar, packed
1 T. cinnamon
4 7-1/2 oz. tubes refrigerated
   biscuits, separated

1/2 c. butter, melted
1/3 c. apple juice
1 t. vanilla extract

Spray a slow cooker with non-stick vegetable spray. In a bowl, mix together sugars and cinnamon. Sprinkle 2 tablespoons in the bottom of slow cooker. Cut biscuits into quarters; coat biscuit pieces with remaining cinnamon-sugar mixture. Add biscuits to slow cooker; sprinkle any extra cinnamon-sugar on top. In a separate bowl, stir together butter, apple juice and vanilla; drizzle over biscuits. Cover and cook on low setting for 2 to 2-1/2 hours. Uncover and let cool for 15 minutes. Turn biscuits out onto a serving platter; cool for several more minutes before serving. Serves 15 to 20.

Christmas
Brunch Menu
Company's Coming
Breakfast Casserole
Aunt June's
Yummy Potatoes
Grandma's Sweet Rolls
Coffee & Juice

Celebrate the season with a holiday brunch buffet for friends and neighbors! Make it casual...guests can come when they can and stay as long as they'd like. It's a joyful time of year to renew old acquaintances while sharing scrumptious food together.

Sleep-Over Breakfast Strata

Emily Martin
Toronto, Ontario

Every year at Christmas, we're sure to have some of my relatives staying for the holidays. All the little cousins beg to sleep around the Christmas tree...Santa has to be very stealthy! In the morning, we share breakfast together before opening our gifts. This recipe fills up our hungry crowd, and everyone loves it.

4 c. day-old white bread, cubed
8 eggs
1-1/2 c. milk
1/2 t. salt
1/2 t. pepper

8-oz. pkg. shredded Cheddar
   cheese
8-oz. pkg. sliced mushrooms
3/4 lb. bacon, crisply cooked
   and crumbled

Place bread in a 6-quart slow cooker sprayed with non-stick vegetable spray; set aside. Beat eggs in a large bowl. Whisk in milk, salt and pepper; stir in cheese and mushrooms. Pour egg mixture evenly over bread; set aside. Cook bacon in a skillet over medium heat until crisp; drain, crumble and sprinkle over top. Cover and cook on low setting for 6 to 8 hours, until eggs have set and top is lightly golden. Uncover and let stand for several minutes before serving. Serves 8 to 10.

Set a mini snowman at each person's place...so sweet! Join two marshmallows with a dab of frosting. Add a gumdrop hat and a tiny scarf cut from fruit leather, then use a toothpick to paint on frosting features.

Brunch Open House

Easy Cheese Soufflé

Elizabeth Blackstone
Racine, WI

Simple and delicious...a staple at our Christmas brunch open house alongside sliced baked ham and golden hashbrowns.

8 slices white bread, crusts
    trimmed, quartered and
    divided
8-oz. pkg. shredded Cheddar
    cheese, divided
4 eggs

1 c. half-and-half or milk
1 c. evaporated milk
1 t. dried parsley
1/4 t. salt
paprika to taste

In a lightly greased slow cooker, layer half each of bread and cheese; repeat layers. In a large bowl, beat together remaining ingredients; pour over top. Cover and cook on low setting for 3 to 4 hours, until set. Serves 4.

For best results when using a slow cooker, be sure the crock is filled at least half full and no more than two-thirds full.

Snow-Day Hot Chocolate

Robin Hill
Rochester, NY

Rich and smooth, this hot chocolate will satisfy grown-ups as well as kids. It's a special treat we share after sledding or ice skating.

14-oz. can sweetened condensed milk
6-oz. pkg. semi-sweet chocolate chips
4 1-oz. sqs. unsweetened baking chocolate, chopped
2 qts. milk, divided
1 T. vanilla extract
Garnish: mini marshmallows or whipped cream

In a 4-quart slow cooker, combine condensed milk and chocolates. Cover and cook on high setting for about 30 minutes, stirring every 10 minutes, until chocolate is melted. Whisk in 2 cups milk until smooth. Gradually stir in remaining milk and vanilla. Cover and cook on high setting for an additional 2 hours, or until heated through. Just before serving, whisk again. Turn slow cooker to low setting to keep warm. To serve, ladle hot chocolate into mugs. Top with marshmallows or a dollop of whipped cream. Serves 15 to 20.

Take the whole family to select and cut a Christmas tree...an old tradition that's worth keeping. Have hot chocolate waiting in a slow cooker to chase away the chill afterwards, with candy-cane stirrers just for fun!

Brunch Open House

Hot Spiced Fruit

Ellie Brandel
Milwaukie, OR

Delicious on its own or served over hot oatmeal for breakfast...
even spooned over ice cream for dessert!

8 Granny Smith or Braeburn
    apples, peeled, cored and
    sliced
8 D'Anjou pears, peeled, cored
    and sliced
1/2 c. raisins
20-oz. can pineapple chunks

1 t. ground cloves
1 t. cinnamon
1 t. nutmeg
2 envs. calorie-free powdered
    sweetener, or sugar to taste
Garnish: whipped topping or
    plain yogurt, nutmeg to taste

Combine apples, pears, raisins and undrained pineapple in a 6-quart slow cooker. Sprinkle with spices and sweetener or sugar; mix gently. Cover and cook on low setting for 8 to 10 hours, until hot and bubbly. Serve warm, garnished with whipped topping or yogurt and a sprinkle of nutmeg. Makes 8 servings.

A place card that doubles as a tree ornament! Paint a wooden holiday cut-out and hand-letter the recipient's name on it. Look for fun shapes like Santas, angels, mittens and stars at craft stores.

Scrambled Eggs Deluxe

Jennie Gist
Gooseberry Patch

*The slow cooker keeps these savory eggs warm until
all the sleepyheads have been fed! I like to serve this with
toasted, buttered English muffins.*

1/2 lb. bacon, cut into
   one-inch pieces
8-oz. pkg. sliced mushrooms
3 T. butter
16 eggs
1 c. milk
1/2 t. salt
1/4 t. pepper

10-3/4 oz. can cream of
   mushroom soup
2 T. fresh chives, chopped
4 roma tomatoes, chopped
   and divided
8-oz. pkg. shredded Cheddar
   cheese, divided

In a skillet over medium heat, cook bacon until crisp; remove bacon
to paper towels. Drain skillet, reserving one tablespoon drippings.
Sauté mushrooms in reserved drippings for 4 to 5 minutes, until
tender. Set aside mushrooms in a bowl. Wipe out skillet with a paper
towel; add butter and melt over medium-low heat. In a large bowl,
beat together eggs, milk, salt and pepper. Add egg mixture to skillet;
lightly scramble eggs until set but still moist. Stir in soup and chives.
Spoon half of egg mixture into a lightly greased slow cooker. Top with
half each of mushrooms, tomatoes, cheese and crumbled bacon; repeat
layers. Cover and cook on low setting for 30 minutes, or until hot and
cheese is melted. May be kept warm on low setting up to 2 hours.
Serves 10 to 12.

Bacon curls make a festive and tasty breakfast plate garnish. Fry bacon
until it's browned but not crisp. Immediately roll up slices and
fasten each with a toothpick.

Brunch Open House

Biscuits & Sausage Gravy

Erin Brock
Charleston, WV

Hearty enough for my hungry boys!

16-oz. pkg. ground pork
    breakfast sausage
2 7-1/2 oz. tubes refrigerated
    biscuits, separated

2 10-3/4 oz. cans cream of
    mushroom soup

Brown sausage in a skillet over medium heat; drain. Arrange half of the biscuits in the bottom of a greased slow cooker. Layer biscuits with half the sausage and one can of soup. Repeat layers. Cover and cook on low setting for 4 hours, or on high setting for 2 hours. Makes 6 to 8 servings.

Down-Home Cheese Grits

Stephanie Mayer
Portsmouth, VA

*I grew up on grits here in Virginia...it's still a must
at family breakfasts! For an extra special brunch dish,
top the cooked grits with sautéed shrimp.*

1-1/2 c. stone-ground grits,
    uncooked
6 c. chicken broth or water
2 t. salt
1/4 c. butter, sliced

2 c. whipping cream or whole
    milk
16-oz. pkg. shredded sharp
    Cheddar cheese
Optional: additional butter

Add grits, broth or water and salt to a lightly greased slow cooker; stir. Cover and cook on low setting for 6 to 8 hours. Shortly before serving time, stir in butter, cream or milk and desired amount of cheese. Cover and let stand several minutes, until cheese is melted. Serve topped with additional butter, if desired. Makes 8 servings.

Cheesy Chicken-Broccoli Quiche

Kendall Hale
Lynn, MA

We enjoy this easy batter-topped quiche for busy weeknight meals as well as weekend holiday brunches.

2 lbs. boneless, skinless chicken breasts
10-oz. pkg. frozen chopped broccoli, thawed
3/4 c. all-purpose flour
3/4 t. baking powder
1/2 t. salt
1 c. evaporated milk
2 eggs
2 T. onion, chopped
2 t. dried parsley
1 c. shredded Cheddar cheese

Coat a slow cooker with non-stick vegetable spray. Arrange chicken in slow cooker; top with broccoli. Cover and cook on low setting for 6 to 8 hours, until chicken is fork-tender. In a bowl, whisk together flour, baking powder, salt, evaporated milk and eggs. Fold in remaining ingredients; pour mixture over broccoli. Increase heat to high; cover and cook for one hour, until set and cheese is melted. Serves 6.

Serve a zingy new fruit drink at breakfast. Mix equal parts chilled pomegranate juice, orange juice and sparkling water. Pour into stemmed glasses over ice...so refreshing!

Brunch Open House

Crustless Mushroom-Swiss Quiche

*Samantha Starks
Madison, WI*

You can speed up the prep time by cooking the bacon, chopping the veggies and assembling the egg mixture ahead of time. Wrap separately and tuck in the fridge until you're ready to fill the crock.

4 slices bacon
1 T. olive oil
16-oz. pkg. mushrooms, chopped
1/2 c. red pepper, chopped
10-oz. pkg. frozen chopped spinach, thawed and very well drained

1-1/2 c. shredded Swiss cheese
8 eggs
2 c. half-and-half or milk
2 T. fresh chives, snipped
1/2 t. salt
1/4 t. pepper
1/2 c. biscuit baking mix

In a skillet over medium heat, cook bacon until crisp; drain on paper towels and crumble. Drain skillet; add oil to skillet and heat over medium heat. Sauté mushrooms and red pepper in oil until tender. Stir in spinach and cheese; remove from heat. In a bowl, beat together eggs, half-and-half or milk, chives, salt and pepper. Stir mushroom mixture into egg mixture. Sprinkle with biscuit mix and stir gently. Pour egg mixture into a lightly greased slow cooker; sprinkle bacon on top. Cover and cook on low setting for 4 to 5 hours, or on high setting for 2 to 2-1/2 hours, until a knife tip inserted into the center tests clean. Let stand for 15 to 30 minutes before serving. Makes 6 to 8 servings.

No time for a leisurely family breakfast? Try serving breakfast for dinner...it's sure to become a family favorite!

Eggnog Bread Pudding

Annette Ingram
Grand Rapids, MI

It's Christmastime...splurge and have dessert for breakfast! I use any leftover eggnog the next day to make scrumptious French toast.

7 eggs
2 c. eggnog
1 c. milk
1/2 c. brown sugar, packed
1 t. vanilla extract
1 T. cinnamon
1/2 t. nutmeg
1 loaf day-old white bread,
   torn into 1-inch pieces
Garnish: additional eggnog or
   light cream, nutmeg to taste

In a large bowl, whisk together all ingredients except bread and garnish. Fold in bread pieces until well coated; spoon into a lightly greased slow cooker. Cover and cook on low setting for 6 to 8 hours, until center is set. Serve warm, topped with eggnog or cream and a sprinkle of nutmeg. Makes 6 to 8 servings.

Little extras for Christmas morning...a small wrapped gift at each place setting, soft holiday music in the background and no lights allowed except those on the tree. So magical!

Brunch Open House

Breakfast Apple Cobbler

Hannah Hopkins
Plainfield, VT

This cobbler is so warm and delicious on a chilly winter morning.

8 Granny Smith apples, peeled,
   cored and sliced
1/2 c. sugar
1/2 t. ground cloves
2/3 t. cinnamon
1/8 t. salt

juice of 1 lemon
1/4 c. butter, melted
2 c. granola cereal
Optional: whipped cream or
   plain yogurt

Place apples in a lightly greased slow cooker; sprinkle with sugar, spices and salt. Drizzle with lemon juice and butter; toss gently to mix. Sprinkle granola over apple mixture. Cover and cook on low setting for 7 to 9 hours, or on high setting for 2 to 3 hours, until apples are tender. Serve warm, topped with whipped cream or yogurt, if desired. Makes 6 to 8 servings.

Serve up cobbler parfaits in mini Mason jars or small glasses. Alternate scoops of warm fruit cobbler and layers of whipped cream. Garnish with a dollop of whipped cream and a sprinkle of cinnamon. Perfect for a brunch buffet!

Eggs Italiana

Mia Rossi
Charlotte, NC

A deliciously different brunch dish.

1/2 lb. thinly sliced provolone
   cheese, divided
10 eggs, beaten
1 c. milk
1/2 t. pepper
1/4 lb. deli sliced prosciutto
   or ham, chopped

1/2 c. roasted red peppers,
   drained and chopped
1/2 c. canned artichokes,
   drained and thinly sliced
1 T. butter, melted

Set aside 3 cheese slices; chop remaining cheese and place in a large
bowl. Add eggs, milk and pepper; whisk well. Stir in remaining
ingredients except butter. Brush a slow cooker with butter. Pour egg
mixture into slow cooker. Cover and cook on low setting for 3 to
3-1/2 hours. Arrange reserved cheese slices on top. Cover and cook
an additional 15 minutes, or just until cheese is melted. Serves 6.

Salt & pepper is a must with breakfast egg and potato dishes.
Bring a little fun to the breakfast table with a pair of
vintage-style "kissing" shakers!

Brunch Open House

Savory Breakfast Casserole

Jessica Shrout
Flintstone, MD

An easy overnight breakfast busy moms will love!

1 lb. ground pork breakfast
   sausage
14 slices bread
Optional: 2 t. mustard
2-1/2 c. shredded Cheddar or
   Monterey Jack cheese

1 doz. eggs, beaten
2-1/4 c. milk
1 t. salt
1 t. pepper

In a skillet over medium heat, cook sausage until browned; drain. Meanwhile, spread bread slices lightly with mustard on one side, if desired; cut or tear bread into quarters. In a greased slow cooker, layer half each of bread, sausage and cheese. Repeat layers. In a large bowl, beat together remaining ingredients; pour over top. Cover and cook on low setting for 8 to 9 hours, until set. Makes 8 servings.

For somehow, not only at Christmas,
But all the year through,
The joy that you give to others
Is the joy that comes back to you.
– John Greenleaf Whittier

Cinnamon-Raisin French Toast

Betty Lou Wright
Hendersonville, TN

Breakfast for supper is so good! This yummy dish smells heavenly while cooking and whets the appetite any time of year.

1 loaf of French or Italian bread,
  cubed and divided
1/2 c. butter, softened
1 c. brown sugar, packed
1-1/2 to 2 t. cinnamon
7 eggs or egg substitute

2-1/2 c. milk
1/2 to 1 t. vanilla extract
1/2 c. raisins, or more to taste
Garnish: maple syrup,
  powdered sugar

Spray a slow cooker with non-stick vegetable spray. Add half of bread to slow cooker; set aside. In a bowl, blend butter, brown sugar and cinnamon. Spoon half of butter mixture over bread layer; place remaining bread on top. In a bowl, whisk together eggs, milk and vanilla; pour over bread. Spread remaining butter mixture on top. Cover and cook on low setting for 4 hours. Gently stir in raisins; cover and cook for an additional hour. At serving time, stir to distribute plumped raisins. Serve warm with maple syrup and/or powdered sugar as desired. Serves 6.

Christmas bazaars are so much fun...jot down the dates on your calendar and invite your girlfriends to come along. These get-togethers are filled with one-of-a-kind handmade items and scrumptious homebaked goodies that are sure to put you in the holiday spirit!

Brunch Open House

Viennese Coffee

Jen Thomas
Santa Rosa, CA

Stir up this flavorful coffee in the crock for your next brunch.

6 c. hot brewed coffee
6 T. chocolate syrup
2 t. sugar
2/3 c. whipping cream
Optional: 1/2 c. creme de cacao

or Irish creme liqueur
Garnish: whipped cream,
   chocolate shavings
   or sprinkles

Combine coffee, chocolate syrup and sugar in a slow cooker. Cover and cook on low setting for 2 to 2-1/2 hours. Stir in cream and liqueur, if using. Cover and cook an additional 30 minutes, or until heated through. Serve coffee in mugs, topped with dollops of whipped cream and garnished as desired. Serves 8 to 10.

Pamper coffee lovers with fresh cream, raw cane sugar and shakers of cinnamon and cocoa. Offer whipped cream for a special treat!

Creamed Chicken For a Crowd

Vickie

A terrific brunch dish! I like to prepare it the day before and refrigerate overnight, then warm it gently in a large saucepan while the biscuits are baking.

8 boneless, skinless chicken
  breasts, cubed
1 t. salt
1/2 t. pepper
2 to 4 T. olive oil, divided
2 white onions, chopped
6 carrots, peeled and thinly
  sliced

2 c. chicken broth, divided
2 to 3 sprigs fresh thyme
1/3 c. butter, softened
3 T. all-purpose flour
12 to 15 biscuits, split

Season chicken with salt and pepper. Heat one tablespoon oil in a skillet over medium heat. Working in batches, cook chicken until golden on all sides, adding another tablespoon of oil oil if needed. Remove chicken to a platter; set aside. Add remaining oil to skillet; cook onions in oil until translucent and lightly golden. Add chicken, carrots and one cup broth to onions. Stir gently and spoon chicken mixture into a lightly greased large slow cooker. Place thyme sprigs on top. Cover and cook on low setting for 5 to 6 hours, until chicken is nearly done. Discard thyme. In a small bowl, blend butter and flour. Add butter mixture and remaining broth to slow cooker; cook and stir until thickened. Increase heat to high; cover and cook for 30 minutes. Season with additional salt and pepper, if desired. To serve, ladle creamed chicken over split biscuits. Serves 12 to 15.

For an extra taste of nostalgia, spoon Creamed Chicken over old-fashioned toast points. Trim the crusts from thinly sliced bread, cut into triangles and bake at 425 degrees until golden, 2 to 3 minutes per side.

Brunch Open House

Scalloped Potatoes & Ham

Kathy Evans
Quinter, KS

This recipe is truly comfort food! My whole family loves it and we seldom have any leftovers. I got the recipe from a local church cookbook and have modified it to suit my family's taste.

2 lbs. cooked ham steaks, cut
    into serving-size pieces
8 potatoes, peeled and sliced
1 onion, sliced

8 slices American cheese
10-3/4 oz. can cream of
    celery soup

Place half of the ham into a slow cooker. Layer with half of the potatoes, then half of the onion. Arrange half of the cheese slices on top, cutting or tearing to fit. Repeat layers. Spread soup over the top. Cover and cook 6 hours on low setting, or 3 hours on high setting, until bubbly and potatoes are tender. Serves 8.

Streamline your holiday plans...ask your family what traditions they most look forward to, including favorite cookies and other festive foods. Then you can focus on tried & true activities, freeing up time to try something new and meaningful to you.

Cinnamon Roll Casserole

Amy Ott
Greenfield, IN

*Ooey-gooey and irresistible! This recipe is great for holiday
mornings...just brew the coffee, serve and enjoy.*

2 12-oz. tubes refrigerated
   cinnamon rolls, separated
4 eggs
1/2 c. whipping cream

3 T. maple syrup
2 t. vanilla extract
1 t. cinnamon
1/4 t. nutmeg

Cover the bottom of a greased slow cooker with cinnamon rolls from
one tube, adding one or 2 more rolls from remaining tube if necessary.
Set aside icing packets. In a bowl, whisk together eggs, cream, maple
syrup, vanilla and spices; drizzle over rolls. Break remaining rolls into
bite-size chunks; place on top. Spoon one packet of icing over top;
refrigerate remaining icing. Cover and cook on low setting for 3 hours,
or until rolls are set. Just before serving, drizzle with remaining icing.
Serves 6 to 8.

For your next brunch, fill sturdy diner-style mugs with ribbon-tied packets
of spiced tea or hot cocoa. Add gift tags that read "Thinking warm thoughts
of you this season." Set a mug at each place setting...they'll serve as
both table decorations and take-home favors.

Brunch Open House

Coconut Pecan Pie Oatmeal

Marsha Baker
Pioneer, OH

What a wonderful way to begin your day, waking up to a hot breakfast waiting for you. This recipe is perfect for Christmas morning or any busy morning during the holiday rush.

1 c. chopped pecans
1/2 c. sweetened flaked coconut
1-1/2 c. long-cooking or steel-
   cut oats, uncooked
4-1/2 c. milk
2/3 c. dark brown sugar, packed

2 T. sugar-free cook & serve
   vanilla pudding mix
1/4 c. butter
1 t. vanilla or coconut extract
Garnish: milk

Place pecans in a small dry skillet over medium heat. Cook until toasted and golden, stirring frequently and watching carefully. Remove pecans to a bowl. Toast coconut in skillet the same way. Reserve half the pecans and coconut for serving. In a slow cooker, combine remaining pecans, coconut and other ingredients; stir. Cover and cook on low setting for 7 to 8 hours. Serve oatmeal in bowls, topped with reserved pecans and coconut and a splash of milk. Makes 5 to 6 servings.

Early in the holiday season, make a list of cookies to bake, cards to write and gifts to buy...even Santa makes a list! Post it on the fridge... you'll be able to check off each item with satisfaction as it's completed.

Country Morning Starter

Christine Camaj
North Salem, NY

This is an easy, hearty breakfast that can cook overnight so it is ready for the next day. I've made it for Thanksgiving and Christmas... Easter too! It is simple and yummy. For a tasty change, use Mexican-blend cheese and serve with salsa.

16-oz. pkg. ground pork
    breakfast sausage
28-oz. pkg. frozen diced
    potatoes
16-oz. pkg. shredded mozzarella
    cheese
10 eggs
3/4 c. milk

1 T. biscuit baking mix or
    pancake mix
1/2 t. nutmeg
1/4 t. salt
1/8 t. pepper
Garnish: additional nutmeg or
    pepper to taste

Brown sausage in a skillet over medium heat. Drain; set aside sausage in a bowl. In same skillet, cook potatoes until lightly golden. Transfer potatoes to a slow cooker coated with non-stick vegetable spray. Top potatoes with sausage and cheese; set aside. In a bowl, whisk together remaining ingredients except garnish. Pour egg mixture over cheese layer; stir gently. Sprinkle additional nutmeg or pepper. Cover and cook on low setting for 6 to 8 hours, until eggs are set. Serves 4 to 6.

Slip jingle bells onto colorful pipe cleaners, then twist into cheery napkin rings...a holly jolly jingle to wake everyone at breakfast!

Brunch Open House

Breakfast Sausage Strata

Nancy Wise
Little Rock, AR

It just takes me a few minutes to pop the ingredients in the slow cooker on Christmas morning, then we open all our gifts. By the time we're finished, breakfast is ready!

10 slices white bread, torn into
   small pieces
14-oz. pkg. mini smoked
   sausages, cut in half if
   desired
9 eggs, beaten well

2-1/4 c. milk
8-oz. pkg. shredded Colby Jack
   or mild Cheddar cheese,
   divided
3/4 t. dry mustard
salt to taste

In a lightly greased slow cooker, layer bread, sausages, half of cheese and seasonings. In a bowl, beat together eggs and milk. Pour egg mixture over top; sprinkle with remaining cheese. Cover and cook on high setting for 1-1/2 to 2 hours, until set. Serves 6 to 8.

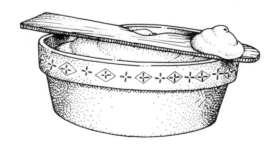

Offer a quick & creamy salmon spread for brunch. Combine an 8-ounce package of cream cheese, 2 tablespoons prepared horseradish, 2 tablespoons chopped fresh dill and salt & pepper to taste. Fold in 1/4 pound of chopped smoked salmon and serve with toasted bagels or crackers.

Apple Oatmeal

Leona Krivda
Belle Vernon, PA

I tried this recipe the first time for a Christmas morning when the family was going to be here. It went over really well and since then I make it often...a good hearty breakfast! Sometimes my hubby & I even have it for dinner when we are busy and tired. We enjoy it with lots of toppings.

4 apples, peeled, cored
   and cubed
1 c. steel-cut oats, uncooked
1/4 c. brown sugar, packed
1 T. flax seed
1-1/2 t. wheat germ
1/2 t. cinnamon
1/4 t. salt

1-1/2 c. milk
1-1/2 c. water
1 t. vanilla extract
1/2 c. sweetened dried cherries
   or other dried fruit
Optional: milk, sliced bananas,
   blueberries, pomegranate
   seeds, pecans

Spray a slow cooker very well with non-stick vegetable spray. Combine apples, oats, brown sugar, flax seed, wheat germ, cinnamon and salt in slow cooker. Add milk, water and vanilla; stir well. Cover and cook on low setting for 5 hours. Add dried fruit; cover and continue cooking for 2 hours. To serve, spoon into bowls; add milk and desired toppings. Cover and refrigerate any leftovers; to serve, microwave until warm. Makes 6 to 8 servings.

Keep both early risers and sleepyheads happy with overnight oatmeal bubbling in the slow cooker. Set out a bowl of brown sugar and a bottle of milk nestled in a bowl of ice...everyone can help just themselves!

Brunch Open House

Overnight Cran-Apple Oatmeal

Lynda Robson
Boston, MA

I love to send the kids off to school on snowy days, knowing they've had a healthy breakfast that will hold them 'til lunch!

8 c. water
2 c. steel-cut oats, uncooked
1 c. apple, peeled, cored and
  chopped
1 c. sweetened dried cranberries

1/4 c. maple syrup
1-1/2 t. cinnamon
Optional: milk, brown sugar,
  chopped nuts

Combine water and oats in a lightly greased slow cooker. Add apple, cranberries, maple syrup and cinnamon; stir. Cover and cook on low setting for 7 to 9 hours. Stir; serve in bowls with milk and desired toppings. Serves 6 to 8.

A sweet favor if children will be coming to your holiday brunch! Fill a basket with little bags of "Reindeer Food" for kids to sprinkle on the lawn on Christmas Eve. To make, simply mix cereal rings with candy sprinkles.

Streusel-Topped Coffee Cake

Penny Sherman
Ava, MO

*Share this tender cake with friends before setting off
for a day of Christmas shopping.*

1-3/4 c. biscuit baking mix,
   divided
3/4 c. sugar
1/2 c. vanilla yogurt
1 egg, beaten

1 t. vanilla extract
1/4 c. brown sugar, packed
1/2 t. cinnamon
1/2 c. powdered sugar
1 to 2 T. milk

Coat a slow cooker with non-stick vegetable spray. Cut a circle of
parchment paper to fit the bottom of the crock; press into place and
spray again. In a bowl, mix 1-1/2 cups biscuit mix, sugar, yogurt, egg
and vanilla until well blended; set aside. In a small bowl, mix brown
sugar, cinnamon and remaining biscuit mix. Spoon half of batter into
slow cooker; sprinkle half of brown sugar mixture on top. Repeat
layers. Place 2 paper towels on top of slow cooker to absorb
condensation. Cover and cook on high setting for 1-3/4 to 2 hours,
until a toothpick inserted in the center tests clean. Let coffee cake stand
in crock for 10 minutes. Turn out onto a plate; peel off parchment
paper. Turn cake over again onto a serving platter, so streusel is on
top. In a separate small bowl, whisk together powdered sugar and
milk, adding enough milk to form a drizzling consistency. Drizzle glaze
over coffee cake. Makes 8 servings.

A tiered cake stand looks inviting and saves table space too! Fill alternate
levels with bite-size goodies and Christmas greenery, tucking in
some shiny ornaments for holiday sparkle.

Brunch Open House

Southern Hospitali-Tea

Tina Wright
Atlanta, GA

I hold a holiday open house every December. As guests come in from the cold, a cup of this hot spiced tea is a sure warmer-upper! It's easy to double in a larger slow cooker too.

6 c. boiling water
4 black tea bags
4-inch cinnamon stick

1 c. orange juice
1/2 c. sugar
2 T. lemon juice

Place tea bags and cinnamon stick in a heat-proof pitcher or bowl. Pour in boiling water; cover and let stand for 10 minutes. Strain tea into a slow cooker, discarding tea bags and cinnamon stick. Stir in remaining ingredients. Cover and cook on low setting for 3 to 4 hours. Makes 6 to 8 servings.

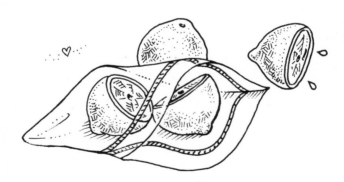

Don't toss that lemon or orange half after it's been juiced! Wrap it and store in the freezer, and it'll be ready to grate whenever a recipe calls for fresh citrus zest.

Cheesy Potatoes

Karen Hazelett
Fremont, IN

A delicious all-occasion dish in the slow cooker! My boss brought in these potatoes for a potluck and everyone wanted the recipe. I've made it several times for weekend guests at our lake home. Add some diced onion or green pepper, if you like.

32-oz. pkg. frozen shredded
   potatoes
10-3/4 oz. can cream of
   mushroom or celery soup

8-oz. container sour cream
16-oz. pkg. shredded Cheddar
   cheese
1/2 c. butter, cubed

Combine all ingredients in a slow cooker sprayed with non-stick vegetable spray. Stir gently. Cover and cook on low setting for 6 hours, until hot and bubbly. Serves 8 to 10.

Go ahead and unpack the Christmas tableware early in December...even the simplest meal is special when served on holly-trimmed plates.

Brunch Open House

Brown Sugar Sausages

Nola Coons
Gooseberry Patch

Serve these sweet sausages at brunch with your fanciest frilled toothpicks...they're really scrumptious!

1 lb. bacon, cut into thirds
14-oz. pkg. mini smoked
   sausages

3/4 c. brown sugar, packed
   and divided

Wrap a piece of bacon around each sausage. Fasten with a wooden toothpick, if desired. Arrange half of bacon-wrapped sausages in a slow cooker. Sprinkle with half of the brown sugar, covering completely. Repeat layers, ending with brown sugar. Cover and cook on low setting for 3 to 4 hours, until bubbly and golden. Serves 8.

Keep it simple on Christmas morning. Instead of preparing a fruit salad, set out a bowl brimming with bright-colored clementines. Kids especially like these juicy little peel & eat oranges!

Quiche Lorraine Bake

Kelly Alderson
Erie, PA

Just a little different from other breakfast casseroles! My daughter helps with the toast while I whip up the eggs. Sometimes I'll replace the ham with crispy bacon. So good!

4 slices white bread, toasted
   and crusts trimmed
4 t. butter, softened
2 c. shredded Swiss cheese,
   divided
1/2 lb. cooked ham, diced
6 eggs

1 c. whipping cream or
   half-and-half
1 T. mayonnaise
1/2 t. Dijon mustard
pepper to taste
Optional: 1/8 t. cayenne pepper

Spread toast slices with butter on one side; tear toast into bite-size pieces. Place toast pieces butter-side down in a slow cooker sprayed with non-stick vegetable spray. Layer with half of the cheese, all of the ham and remaining cheese. In a bowl, beat together remaining ingredients; pour over cheese. Cover and cook on high setting for 2 hours, or until eggs are set. Serves 6 to 8.

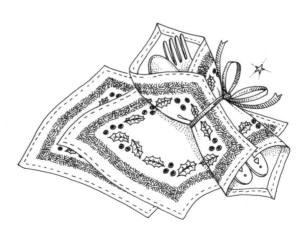

Whip up a batch of napkins from cotton fabric in a cheery holiday print. Cut fabric into 12-inch squares or even 18-inch squares for lap-size napkins, then finish with a simple hem or even fringed edges. So easy!

Festive Fuss-Free
Party Food

Mom's Hot Turkey Sandwiches

Katie Majeske
Denver, PA

These sandwiches are so good...the recipe has been in our family for a long time! They're always a hit, and they're easy to make. Often I'll buy a turkey breast and roast it so I can prepare this the following day.

8 c. cooked turkey, cubed
1 to 1-1/2 c. pasteurized process
    cheese spread, cubed
1 c. turkey or chicken broth

10-3/4 oz. can cream of
    mushroom or chicken soup
12 to 16 sandwich buns, split

Combine all ingredients except buns in a large slow cooker. Cover and cook on low setting for 3 to 4 hours, until bubbly and cheese is melted. Stir; spoon onto buns. Makes 12 to 16 servings.

Slow cookers make it easy to whip up tender, juicy sandwiches for a crowd. They're super party helpers too...large crocks can keep warm beverages piping hot, while mini crocks keep dips bubbly and delicious.

Festive Fuss-Free Party Food

Teriyaki Steak Subs

Virginia Watson
Scranton, PA

*We really enjoy these sandwiches at all our winter
tailgating parties. They're great for an easy dinner too.*

1/2 c. onion, chopped
1/2 c. soy sauce
1/4 c. red wine or beef broth
1 T. fresh ginger, peeled
   and grated
2 t. garlic, minced

1 T. sugar
3 lbs. beef round steak, cut
   crosswise into thirds
8 to 10 sub buns, split
Garnish: thinly sliced onion

In a bowl, combine all ingredients except beef, buns and garnish.
Layer beef pieces in a slow cooker, spooning some of the onion
mixture over each piece. Cover and cook on low setting for 6 to
7 hours, until beef is tender. Remove beef to a platter, reserving
cooking liquid in slow cooker. Let beef stand several minutes before
thinly slicing. To serve, place sliced beef on buns; top with sliced onion
and some of the reserved cooking liquid. Makes 8 to 10 servings.

It's fun to hang little unexpected surprises from the dining room chandelier.
Start with a swag of greenery, then tuck in Christmas whimsies like
glass balls, tiny snowmen, cookie cutters and smiling Santas.

Juiciest BBQ Pulled Pork

Emily Hartzell
Portland, IN

Depending on where you live, you'll have a different preference of how to serve pulled pork sandwiches. Try this delicious recipe all different ways...no barbecue sauce, extra sauce, sprinkled with hot pepper sauce or topped with coleslaw!

7 to 8-lb. pork butt or shoulder
　　roast, trimmed
4 to 5 T. dry rub for pork
1 onion, sliced
1/2 c. cider vinegar
2 c. apple juice

20-oz. bottle barbecue sauce
10 to 12 buns, split
Optional: additional barbecue
　　sauce, hot pepper sauce,
　　coleslaw

Pat pork dry with paper towels; generously apply dry rub all over. Place pork in a large pan; cover and refrigerate for 8 to 24 hours. Cover the bottom of a large slow cooker with onion slices. Place pork on top; drizzle with vinegar and apple juice. Cover and cook on low setting for about 10 hours. Check on liquid levels occasionally, removing some of the cooking liquid if necessary to prevent overflowing. When pork is fork-tender, remove pork and onion to a large bowl, reserving one to 2 cups of cooking liquid. Discard remaining liquid. Let pork stand until cool enough to handle. Shred pork, discarding any bones and gristle. Stir in barbecue sauce and return pork to slow cooker. Cover and cook on low setting for about one hour, until warmed through, adding some of the reserved cooking liquid if pork is getting too dry. Serve pork in buns, garnished as desired.

Homemade sweet potato chips...yum! Peel sweet potatoes, slice thinly, toss with oil and spread on a baking sheet. Place on the center oven rack and bake at 400 degrees for 22 to 25 minutes, turning once. Sprinkle with cinnamon-sugar and serve warm.

Festive Fuss-Free Party Food

Chip-Chop Ham

Carlyn Kamann
Sandusky, OH

Christmas Eve at my parents' house always included an evening meal of these slow-cooker sandwiches and Christmas cookies. Our favorite sandwich was also the easiest to prepare! Enjoy...you'll be back for seconds!

2 lbs. deli chip-chop ham
2-ltr. bottle ginger ale

8 soft buns, split
Garnish: mustard

Place ham in a slow cooker. Pour in enough ginger ale to cover ham plus one more cup of ginger ale. Cover and cook on high setting for 2 hours, until heated through. Turn to low setting to keep ham warm for serving. Lift out ham with a fork onto buns; top with mustard. Makes 8 servings.

Make holiday entertaining extra easy with an all-appetizers party instead of a sit-down dinner! Set up tables in different areas so guests can mingle as they enjoy yummy spreads and finger foods. Your get-together is sure to be a festive success.

Soy & Honey Chicken Wings

Lynn Williams
Muncie, IN

A must at our family's annual holiday get-together!

3 lbs. chicken wings
salt and pepper to taste
1-1/2 c. honey
1/2 c. soy sauce

2 T. oil
2 T. catsup
1 clove garlic, minced

Season wings with salt and pepper. Place wings in a lightly greased large slow cooker. In a bowl, combine remaining ingredients; mix well and pour evenly over wings. Cover and cook on low setting for 6 to 8 hours, until wings are glazed and chicken juices run clear when pierced. Serves 6 to 8.

No peeking! That's good advice for gift packages and slow cookers alike.
Cooking time increases by 15 to 20 minutes every time a
slow cooker's lid is lifted.

Festive Fuss-Free Party Food

Italian Mushrooms

Thomas Campbell
Eden Prairie, MN

This is a take on a recipe from my sister in-law. She uses ranch dressing mix, while I like the zest of the Italian dressing. Whenever I double the recipe, I like to use one packet each of zesty and regular Italian dressing.

4 lbs. small whole mushrooms, trimmed
2 c. butter, cut into thirds

0.7-oz. pkg. regular or zesty Italian salad dressing mix

Place mushrooms in a slow cooker; top with butter and seasoning mix. Cover and cook on high setting for 3 to 4 hours, stirring occasionally. Turn slow cooker to low setting to keep mushrooms warm. Serve with toothpicks. Makes 8 to 10 servings.

Barbecued Water Chestnuts

Betty Gretch
Owendale, MI

I got this recipe from a favorite aunt who serves these tasty morsels for the holidays. They're good for game-time appetizers too... I always bring home an empty dish!

2 8-oz. cans whole water chestnuts, drained
1 lb. bacon, cut in half

1-1/2 c. catsup
6 T. brown sugar, packed
1 T. vinegar

Wrap each chestnut in a piece of bacon; fasten with a wooden toothpick. Place on an aluminum foil-lined baking sheet. Bake at 350 degrees for 30 minutes, or until crisp and golden. Remove chestnuts to a mini slow cooker; set aside. Combine remaining ingredients in a saucepan over medium-low heat. Bring to a simmer; cook for 15 minutes, or until thickened. Spoon sauce over chestnuts. Turn slow cooker to low setting for serving. Serves 10.

For a reminder that Santa's on his way, wire a length of sleigh bells to a fresh greenery wreath...a jolly jingle every time the door opens!

Mom's Best Hot Cheese Dip

Tracee Cummins
Amarillo, TX

For as long as I can remember, my mother has made this fabulous dip every Christmas. When I was little, she made it in a chafing dish...I was always fascinated by the blue flame under the pan! Nowadays she makes it in a slow cooker for ease of preparation as well as portability. This hearty dip is perfect to make ahead for any occasion that needs a little spice!

1 lb. pasteurized process cheese spread, sliced or cubed
1 lb. sharp Cheddar cheese, sliced
10-3/4 oz. can chicken gumbo soup, drained

16-oz. jar red taco sauce (not salsa)
8-oz. can chopped green chiles
chopped onion to taste
corn or tortilla chips

Combine all ingredients except corn or tortilla chips in a slow cooker. Cover and cook on low setting, stirring often, until melted and smooth, about 45 minutes. Serve warm with corn or tortilla chips. Serves 10 to 12.

A mug tree from the kitchen makes a clever holder for displaying several favorite Christmas ornaments...perfect for a party table or buffet.

Festive Fuss-Free Party Food

Easy Cheesy Chili Dogs

Teri Lindquist
Gurnee, IL

One day I grabbed these ingredients in my pantry, put them in my slow cooker, and in two hours, we had a fun and delicious meal! I was pleasantly surprised to see that the saucy mixture stays nice and thick. Now I keep these ingredients on hand all the time. If you're feeding a crowd, the chili mixture is plenty for two packages of hot dogs without having to double the other ingredients.

1 lb. hot dogs
15-oz. can chili
15-oz. can black beans, drained
    and rinsed
10-3/4 oz. can Cheddar
    cheese soup

4-oz. can diced green chiles,
    drained
8 to 10 hot dog buns, split
Optional: chopped tomato,
    diced onion, sour cream

Place hot dogs in a slow cooker; set aside. In a bowl, stir together chili, beans, soup and chiles; spoon over hot dogs. Cover and cook on low setting for about 2 hours, stirring occasionally, until hot and bubbly. Serve hot dogs and sauce on buns, adding toppings as desired. Makes 8 to 10 servings.

Alongside each slow cooker, use wooden alphabet tiles to spell out recipe names. Guests will know just what's inside, and it's a fun twist on the traditional table tent.

Creamy Spinach Dip

Jessica Payne
Springville, TN

*I love to make finger foods and snacks on Sundays for
my husband to take to work for break during the week.
This creamy dip is his favorite!*

10-oz. pkg. frozen spinach
16-oz. pkg. queso-style
   pasteurized processed cheese
   spread, cubed

8-oz. pkg. cream cheese, cubed
   and softened
1/4 c. milk
tortilla chips

Place spinach in a saucepan; add enough water to half-cover. Cook
over medium heat until spinach starts to thaw. Drain spinach well;
remove to a slow cooker. Add cheeses, Special Seasoning and milk.
Cover and cook on low setting for one to 2 hours, until cheeses are
melted. Stir until smooth. Serve warm with tortilla chips. Serves
10 to 12.

Special Seasoning:

1 T. Italian seasoning
2 t. onion powder
2 t. garlic powder
1 t. salt

1 t. pepper
1/2 t. cayenne pepper
1/2 t. paprika

Combine all ingredients in a small bowl.

The roads of life lead us away,
But wherever we may roam
Christmas memories take us back
And Christmas roads lead home.
    – Edyth M. Groves

Festive Fuss-Free Party Food

Tuscan White Bean Spread

Marlene Darnell
Newport Beach, CA

*This savory, healthy spread is sure to be welcome
at your next holiday get-together.*

4 15-oz. cans cannellini beans,
    drained and rinsed
1 onion, chopped
4 cloves garlic, chopped
2 T. extra-virgin olive oil

1 c. water
1 t. dried rosemary
1 t. red pepper flakes
1 t. salt
1 t. pepper

Combine all ingredients in a slow cooker; stir. Cover and cook on high
setting for 3 hours, or on low setting for 5 hours. Serve warm with
Savory Crostini. Makes 10 to 12 servings.

Savory Crostini:

1 to 2 French baguettes, sliced
2 cloves garlic, halved

2 T. olive oil

Rub each baguette slice with the cut side of a garlic clove. Arrange on
an ungreased baking sheet; drizzle with oil. Bake at 400 degrees for
5 to 8 minutes, until golden. Let cool before serving.

If you have friends who live far away, gather together your family and
hold up a big sign that says "Merry Christmas!" Take a picture
and send it to them...they'll love it!

Pulled Pork & Peppers

April Cadeau
Mississauga, Ontario

My husband, two sons and I had just moved north during a cold winter. I found this was a meal I could start in the morning before going to work. When I came home, the house would smell yummy, as my sons would say, and dinner would be ready to serve. What could be better?

5-lb. pork roast
1 t. chili powder
salt and pepper to taste
14-1/2 oz. can stewed tomatoes
4 to 5 pickled banana peppers,
   sliced
3 red peppers, sliced

12-oz. bottle regular or
   non-alcoholic beer
1/4 c. hickory-flavored barbecue
   sauce
8 to 12 sandwich buns, split
Optional: shredded Cheddar
   cheese

Trim off most of the fat on the pork, leaving a little for flavor. Season with chili powder, salt and pepper; place in a large slow cooker. Top pork with remaining ingredients except buns and cheese. Cover and cook on low setting for 6 to 7 hours, until pork is very tender. Shred pork with 2 forks, discarding any bones. Cooking liquid may be reserved for dipping. Serve shredded pork on buns, topped with cheese, if desired. Makes 8 to 12 servings.

Turn your favorite shredded pork and beef into party food, meatballs too.
Serve up bite-size portions on slider buns. Guests will love sampling
a little of everything.

Festive Fuss-Free Party Food

BBQ Ranch Chicken Buns

Cris Goode
Mooresville, IN

*We love this super-simple recipe and leftovers can be used in
so many ways...on tacos, more sandwiches or even pizza!*

8 boneless, skinless chicken
   thighs
seasoned salt to taste
1 c. barbecue sauce

8 sandwich buns, split
Garnish: additional barbecue
   sauce, ranch salad dressing

Place chicken in a large slow cooker. Sprinkle generously with
seasoned salt; pour barbecue sauce on top. Cover and cook on low
setting for 5 to 6 hours, or on high setting for 3 to 4 hours, until
chicken is very tender. Remove chicken to a large bowl; shred with
2 forks. Serve shredded chicken on buns, drizzled with barbecue sauce
and ranch dressing. Makes 8 servings.

As Christmas nears, plan a family slumber party! Set up quilts and
sleeping bags around the tree, pass around lots of snacks and watch a
holiday movie together. Before drifting off to sleep, read "The Night
Before Christmas" with only the tree lights on.

Hot Brats

Barbara Imler
Noblesville, IN

*The guys really like these tasty sausage bites and make sure
I never have any leftovers! This recipe is so easy to prepare
and to carry to gatherings right in the slow cooker.*

2 to 2-1/2 lbs. bratwurst,
   knockwurst or Polish
   pork sausage, cut into
   1-inch pieces
2 T. oil
12-oz. can regular or
   non-alcoholic beer

1/3 c. brown sugar, packed
2 T. cornstarch
1/3 c. vinegar
1/4 c. prepared horseradish
1/4 c. mustard

In a large skillet over medium-high heat, brown sausage in oil. Drain;
add beer to skillet. Cover and simmer for 10 minutes. Meanwhile, in a
small bowl, combine brown sugar and cornstarch; blend in vinegar,
horseradish and mustard. Add mixture to sausages. Cover and cook
until thickened and bubbly, stirring frequently. To serve, transfer to
a slow cooker on low setting. Makes about 8 servings.

Need a tree skirt? A jolly vintage Christmas tablecloth with its brightly
colored images of Santas, elves or carolers is easily wrapped around
the tree for a bit of old-fashioned holiday fun.

Festive Fuss-Free Party Food

Italian Beef Sandwiches

Cynthia Johnson
Verona, WI

This is my go-to recipe to feed a crowd...everyone loves it!

3 to 4-lb. boneless beef
   rump roast
10-1/2 oz. can French
   onion soup
1 c. beef broth
2 cloves garlic, minced

0.7-oz. pkg. Italian salad
   dressing mix
8 to 10 sandwich buns, split
Optional: sliced Provolone
   cheese

Place beef in a large slow cooker; set aside. In a bowl, combine remaining ingredients except buns and cheese; pour over beef. Cover and cook on low setting for 9 to 10 hours, until very tender. Shred beef with 2 forks. Serve beef on buns, topped with a cheese slice, if desired. Makes 8 to 10 servings.

Shredded Beef Sandwiches

Julie Jayjohn
Miamisburg, OH

It is our Christmas Eve tradition to have these sandwiches with other side dishes...delicious!

10-3/4 oz. can cream of
   celery soup
1.35-oz. pkg. onion soup mix

3 lbs. lean stew beef cubes
10 to 12 sandwich buns, split

Pour soup into a slow cooker; add soup mix and stir well. Add beef; do not stir. Cover and cook on high setting for 6 to 7 hours. Mix and shred beef well with a potato masher and a fork. Serve beef on buns. Makes 10 to 12 servings.

Slow-cooked roast beef sandwiches are so deliciously juicy! To keep that juice from dripping, wrap individual servings in aluminum foil, then peel back as they're eaten.

Hot Crab Dip

Michelle Hogan
Huntington, IN

When I bring this appetizer to office carry-ins, it is gone in an instant! People actually beg me to bring this in from time to time. Don't be tempted to use canned crabmeat, as the consistency won't be as good.

16-oz. pkg. imitation flake-style
   crabmeat, chopped
2 8-oz. pkgs. cream cheese,
   cubed

1/2 c. butter, sliced
1 T. fresh chives, chopped
2 T. Worcestershire sauce
crackers or bread slices

Combine all ingredients except crackers or bread in a slow cooker. Cover and cook on high setting for 2 hours, stirring after one hour. Stir again. Serve warm with crackers or bread. Makes 20 servings.

Host a gift wrapping party! Gather up giftwrap, scissors and tape, play cheerful Christmas music and set out some light refreshments for nibbling. With everyone helping each other, you'll be done in a snap!

Festive Fuss-Free Party Food

Warm Seafood Dip

Carol Aguilar
Tucson, AZ

*During the holidays, I like to use the multi-colored tortilla chips
for dipping to make it more festive!*

2 8-oz. pkgs. cream cheese,
   cubed
1/2 lb. tiny shrimp
1/4 lb. imitation crabmeat,
   flaked

1 T. lemon juice
1 t. Worcestershire sauce
1 t. garlic, minced
tortilla chips

Combine all ingredients except tortilla chips in a slow cooker. Cover
and cook on high setting for 30 minutes, or until cheese melts; stir.
Turn slow cooker to low setting; cover and cook for one hour. Stir
again. Serve warm with tortilla chips. Makes 15 servings.

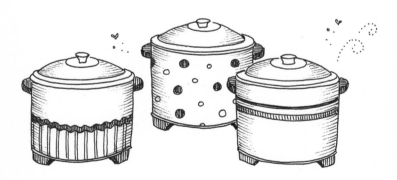

Bring the whole neighborhood together with a progressive dinner! Start at
one end of the street with slow-cooker appetizers...finish at the other end
with desserts. With crocks of prepared food set on low or warm, everyone
can go from house to house without missing any of the fun or food.

Old English Wassail

Sherry Tysinger
Painesville, OH

I attended Milligan College where we had Madrigal dinners every Christmas. Just like merry old England, we had English dishes, strolling minstrel players and singers. One item on the menu was Wassail, a warm spiced drink that's become a family favorite. We still make it for gatherings around the holidays.

1 gal. apple cider or apple juice
2 12-oz. cans frozen orange-
    pineapple juice, thawed
2 c. water

2 T. red cinnamon candies
4 to 6 4-inch cinnamon sticks
Optional: unpeeled orange,
    whole cloves

Combine all ingredients in a large slow cooker. If desired, stud an unpeeled orange with cloves; add to slow cooker. Cover and cook on low setting for 2 to 3 hours, until hot. Makes 20 to 25 servings.

Throw a caroling party. Make up hand-outs with lyrics, or stick to favorites like "Jingle Bells" that everybody is sure to know. Serenade your neighbors, a nursing home or hospital, then end the evening with hot cider and cookies at your home. Sure to be lots of fun!

Festive Fuss-Free Party Food

Spiced & Sugared Nuts

Charmie Fisher
Fontana, CA

I love to make these nuts all year long! It's just so easy using a slow cooker. Great for gifts and for topping desserts. My favorite way, though, to use them is as a topping for a crisp green salad...people just oooh and ahhh over it! As an added bonus, your house smells wonderful while they're cooking.

1 lb. walnut halves, pecan
   halves or whole almonds
1/2 c. butter, melted
1/2 c. powdered sugar

1-1/2 t. cinnamon
1/4 t. allspice
1/4 t. ground ginger
1/8 t. ground cloves

Preheat slow cooker on high setting for 15 minutes. Add nuts; drizzle with butter and stir until well blended. Add powdered sugar, stirring until nuts are coated. Cover and cook on high setting for 15 minutes. Reduce heat to low setting. Remove lid and cook, uncovered, for about 2 hours, stirring occasionally, until nuts are coated with a crisp glaze. Transfer nuts to a bowl. Combine spices in a cup; sift over nuts, stirring to coat evenly. Let cool before serving; store in a covered container. Makes about one pound.

Spiced & Sugared Nuts are delicious sprinkled on a cold-weather salad
of chopped apples or pears, blue cheese crumbles and lettuce.
Drizzle with poppy seed dressing.

Mapley Appetizers

Lynnette Jones
East Flat Rock, NC

With traditional Christmas colors from the green pepper and the red maraschino cherries, this is a wonderful holiday appetizer. The recipe was passed down to me by my husband's aunt.

15-1/4 oz. can pineapple tidbits,
   drained and juice reserved
1/2 c. maple syrup
1/2 c. vinegar
1/3 c. water
4 t. cornstarch

14-oz. pkg. mini smoked
   sausages
2/3 c. green pepper, cut into
   1" squares
1/2 c. maraschino cherries

In a bowl, blend reserved pineapple juice, maple syrup, vinegar and water; stir in cornstarch. Pour into a slow cooker. Add pineapple and remaining ingredients; stir gently. Cover and cook on low setting for 4 to 6 hours. Serves 8 to 10.

Wrap toss pillows in holiday fabric and tie with brightly colored ribbons just like gift packages! Add a few stitches or tiny safety pins to hold the ribbons in place.

Festive Fuss-Free Party Food

Hawaiian Meatballs

Teri Lindquist
Gurnee, IL

This recipe came about when I needed an appetizer and wanted to use items I had on hand. Now it is one of my most requested recipes, and no one can believe it has only three ingredients! Try it with cocktail sausages too.

2 16-oz. pkgs. frozen meatballs   8-oz. bottle barbecue sauce
10-oz. jar pineapple preserves

Place meatballs in a slow cooker. In a bowl, stir together preserves and sauce; pour over meatballs. Gently stir to combine. Cover and cook on low setting for 2 to 3 hours, stirring gently once or twice, until meatballs are hot. Serve with toothpicks. Makes 10 servings.

Tipsy Meatballs

Kathy Grashoff
Fort Wayne, IN

This recipe is so quick, yet gets rave reviews at holiday parties. My daughter-in-law always takes home the leftovers...if there are any!

2 16-oz. pkgs. frozen meatballs   3/4 c. whiskey bourbon or
1 c. catsup   apple juice
1 c. dark brown sugar, packed

Place meatballs in a slow cooker. In a bowl, stir together remaining ingredients; pour over meatballs. Stir gently. Cover and cook on low setting for 2 to 3 hours, until meatballs are hot. Stir again. Serve with toothpicks. Serves 10.

Get the family together for a photo with Santa...sure to make big and little kids giggle!

Cheryl's Awesome Artichoke Dip

Judy Taylor
Butler, MO

So simple to make, and so wonderful to eat, I'm so glad this recipe was shared with me! A small package of frozen chopped spinach may be thawed and added, if desired. Be sure to drain it well.

1 c. sour cream
1 c. mayonnaise
14-oz. can artichokes, drained
   and finely chopped

6-oz. pkg. shredded Parmesan
   cheese
1 t. garlic, minced
crackers or bread slices

Mix together all ingredients in a mini slow cooker. Cover and cook on high setting for one to 2 hours, until bubbly and cheese has melted. Serve warm with crackers or bread for dipping. Makes 8 to 10 servings.

Not sure if your old slow cooker is still working as it should? It's simple to check. Fill it 2/3 full of water, cover and cook on high setting for 4 hours. Check water with an instant-read thermometer...if it reads 180 degrees, it's good to go.

Festive Fuss-Free Party Food

Chicken Wing Dip

Terri Scungio
Williamsburg, VA

This recipe was given to me by a friend many years ago, and it is the real deal! If you are a true western New Yorker, then you know the blue cheese dressing is a must.

1 lb. boneless, skinless chicken
    breasts, cooked and
    shredded
1 c. cayenne hot pepper sauce
1 c. blue cheese salad dressing

8-oz. pkg. cream cheese,
    softened
1 c. shredded mozzarella cheese
carrot and celery sticks, crackers

In a bowl, mix together shredded chicken and hot sauce; set aside. In a separate bowl, mix together salad dressing and cream cheese. Stir in mozzarella cheese and shredded chicken mixture. Transfer mixture to a mini slow cooker. Cover and cook on low setting for 2-1/2 to 3 hours, until heated through and cheese is melted. Serve with carrot and celery sticks and crackers. Serves 6 to 8.

Having a potluck party? Ask everyone ahead of time to share the recipe they'll be bringing. Make copies of all the recipes and staple into a booklet...a thoughtful party souvenir!

Plum Good Sausages & Meatballs

Athena Colegrove
Big Springs, TX

One year we received a gift basket of fancy jams & jellies.
What to do with the plum preserves...into the slow cooker
it went! These are sweet and zingy.

18-oz. bottle barbecue sauce
12-oz. jar plum preserves
16-oz. pkg. frozen meatballs

14-oz. pkg. mini smoked
sausages

Combine sauce and preserves in a slow cooker; stir well. Add meatballs and sausages, stirring to coat. Cover and cook on low setting for 5 to 6 hours, or on high setting for 2-1/2 to 3 hours. Serve with toothpicks. Makes 12 servings.

Add pizazz to an appetizer tray...glue tiny, sparkly Christmas balls
onto long toothpicks for serving.

Festive Fuss-Free Party Food

Cranberry Meatballs

Deb Lazarczyk
West Allis, WI

A special aunt shared this recipe with me. She always made her meatballs from scratch, but over the years, I have replaced her homemade meatballs with frozen meatballs to save time. They're still delicious!

3 16-oz. pkgs. frozen meatballs
14-1/2 oz. can sauerkraut
14-oz. can whole-berry
   cranberry sauce

12-oz. jar chili sauce
1/4 c. brown sugar, packed

Place meatballs in a large slow cooker; set aside. In a bowl, stir together undrained sauerkraut and remaining ingredients; pour over meatballs. Cover and cook on high setting for 4 to 5 hours, until hot. Serves 12 to 15.

A length of wire makes it easy to secure evergreen branches to a mailbox. Use chenille stems to wire on berry bunches and a bow, then tuck in a surprise for the letter carrier!

Ski Club Cheddar Fondue

April Jacobs
Loveland, CO

*When I was in college, I went on a ski trip with my friends. I loved
the food in the lodge more than the actual skiing! Fondue was
one of my favorites...with this recipe I can share it anytime.*

12-oz. pkg. shredded sharp
   Cheddar cheese
12-oz. pkg. shredded Gruyère
   cheese

3 T. all-purpose flour
1/8 t. nutmeg
1 c. white wine or chicken broth
cut-up vegetables, bread cubes

Place cheeses in a slow cooker. Sprinkle with flour and nutmeg; toss to
coat. Sprinkle wine over cheese mixture. Cover and cook on high
setting for 45 minutes to one hour, until cheeses melt. Stir. Turn slow
cooker to low setting for serving. Serve with vegetables and bread
cubes for dipping. Makes about 15 servings.

This veggie-packed topiary will certainly "spruce" up your buffet table!
Cover a 12-inch styrofoam cone with aluminum foil. Attach broccoli flowerets
and cherry tomatoes by sticking one end of a toothpick into the veggie and
the other end into the cone. Garnish with cheese "ornaments" cut out
with mini cookie cutters...clever!

Festive Fuss-Free Party Food

Apricot Brie Dip

Emma Brown
Humboldt, Saskatchewan

Creamy and sweet..sure to be a hit at your next party!

1/2 c. dried apricots, finely
    chopped
1/4 c. apricot nectar or
    apple juice
1/3 c. plus 1 T. apricot
    preserves, divided

2-lb. Brie cheese round, rind
    removed and cubed
bread slices or crackers,
    cut-up vegetables

Combine apricots, nectar or juice and 1/3 cup preserves in a slow
cooker. Cover and cook on high setting for 30 to 40 minutes, until hot.
Stir in cheese. Cover and cook on high setting an additional 30 to
40 minutes, until cheese is melted. Stir in remaining preserves. Turn
slow cooker to low setting for serving. Serve with bread or crackers
and vegetables for dipping. Serves 12.

Stack ribbon-tied bundles of sweetly scented candles in
a basket near the front door...a pretty decoration that doubles
as gifts for surprise visitors.

Cinnamon White Cocoa

Jessica Shrout
Flintstone, MD

Growing up, we always knew that after a day of sledding and playing in the snow we would warm up with mugs of hot cocoa. This recipe is not your typical cocoa, but it's a hit with kids and adults alike.

2 qts. milk
8 4-inch cinnamon sticks
2-1/4 c. white chocolate chips
1/4 c. dark brown sugar, packed
4 t. vanilla extract

4 t. cinnamon
1/8 t. salt
Garnish: marshmallow creme,
 caramel topping,
 chopped pecans

Pour milk into a slow cooker; add cinnamon sticks. Cover and cook on low setting for 1-1/2 to 2 hours. Discard cinnamon sticks; add chocolate chips, brown sugar, vanilla and cinnamon. Cover and cook for 30 to 45 minutes. When chocolate chips start to melt, whisk until blended; stir in salt. Cover and cook for an additional 30 minutes. Just before serving, whisk again. Ladle into mugs; garnish as desired. Makes 8 servings.

Family photos make terrific gift tags. Just copy, cut out and tie on.
There's no need to write "To" on each tag...everyone can open
the packages with their picture!

Festive Fuss-Free Party Food

Festive Cranberry Warmer

Donna Wilson
Maryville, TN

This is a wonderful hot beverage we always have on hand for company over the holidays. Everyone likes it.

2 14-oz. cans jellied
    cranberry sauce
4 c. pineapple juice
4 c. water

3/4 c. brown sugar, packed
1 t. pumpkin pie spice
4-inch cinnamon stick

Pour cranberry sauce into a slow cooker; mash with a potato masher. Add pineapple juice, water, brown sugar and spice; whisk well. Add cinnamon stick. Cover and cook on low setting for 2 to 3 hours, until heated through. At serving time, discard cinnamon stick; whisk again. Makes 10 servings.

A large clear glass bowl is a must for entertaining family & friends. Serve up a layered salad, a fruity punch or a sweet dessert trifle...even fill it with shiny glass ornaments to serve as a sparkly centerpiece.

Savory Parmesan Crunch Mix

Tonya Shepphard
Galveston, TX

This taste-tempting snack mix is my family's pick for munching as we watch our favorite Christmas movies. Everyone has their own special bits that they like to pick out and eat. Sure, I could make it in the oven, but this way I can just set it and forget it.

3 c. bite-size crispy corn or
   rice cereal squares
2 c. oyster crackers
2 c. plain bagel chips, broken
   in half
1-1/2 c. mini pretzel twists

1 c. shelled pistachio nuts
2 T. grated Parmesan cheese
1/4 c. butter, melted
1-oz. pkg ranch salad
   dressing mix
1/2 t. garlic powder

In a large slow cooker, combine cereal, crackers, chips, pretzels, nuts and cheese; stir gently and set aside. In a small bowl, stir together remaining ingredients. Drizzle butter mixture over cereal mixture; toss lightly to coat. Cover and cook on low setting for 3 hours. Uncover; stir gently. Cook, uncovered, for an additional 30 minutes. Cool completely; store in an airtight container. Makes about 9 cups.

Paper baking cups are perfect for serving up party-size scoops of nuts or snack mix. They come in lots of colors and patterns too...you're sure to find one to suit your occasion.

Festive Fuss-Free Party Food

Smoky-Good Snack Mix

Darrell Lawry
Kissimmee, FL

This tasty recipe really makes a lot...perfect if you've got loads of friends or co-workers to gift!

4 c. bite-size crispy corn
  cereal squares
3 c. roasted whole almonds
10-oz. pkg. oyster crackers
9-oz. pkg. baked cheese
  snack crackers

1/2 c. butter, melted
2 T. smoke-flavored cooking
  sauce
1 T. Worcestershire sauce
1 t. seasoned salt

In a large slow cooker, combine cereal, almonds and crackers; set aside. In a small bowl, stir together remaining ingredients. Drizzle butter mixture over cereal mixture; toss to coat. Cook, uncovered, on high setting for 2-1/2 hours, stirring every 30 minutes. Cool completely; store in an airtight container. Makes about 17 cups.

Who wouldn't love to receive a movie bucket for Christmas? Decorate a new white paper paint bucket from the hardware store, then fill it with packages of microwave popcorn and other treats. Tuck in a couple of movies on DVD for a gift that will long be remembered!

Chicken Fajitas

Stephanie Carlson
Sioux Falls, SD

*This is one of our family favorites. I love it because it's
hearty, quick & easy...fun to serve at parties too! Boneless beef
can also be prepared this way.*

2 lbs. skinless, boneless
  chicken breasts
1 onion, sliced and separated
  into rings
1 to 2 green peppers, sliced
  into strips
1 to 2 cloves garlic, minced
1 T. dried cilantro
1 t. chili powder
1 t. ground coriander

1 t. salt
1/4 c. lime juice
16-oz. jar salsa
fajita-size flour tortillas, warmed
Garnish: chopped tomatoes,
  sliced black olives, sliced
  avocado, shredded lettuce,
  shredded Cheddar cheese,
  salsa, guacamole, sour cream

Place chicken in a large slow cooker. Top with onion, green pepper and
garlic; aside. Mix seasonings in a small bowl; sprinkle over chicken
and vegetables. Drizzle with lime juice; spoon salsa over top. Cover
and cook on low setting for 6 to 8 hours, until chicken juices run clear
when pierced. Remove chicken to a plate; shred with 2 forks. Stir
chicken into vegetable mixture in slow cooker. To serve, spoon
chicken and vegetables into warmed flour tortillas; add desired
toppings. Serves 4 to 6.

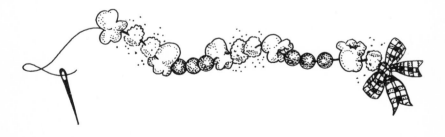

Waxed dental floss is super for stringing old-fashioned garlands of
cranberries and popcorn. It's stronger than regular thread and
the waxed coating slides right through...give it a try!

Festive Fuss-Free Party Food

French Dip

Kathy Walstrom
Glenview, IL

This is an easy and delicious French Dip sandwich. Beer adds a depth of flavor to the au jus that shouldn't be missed.

4-lb. beef rump roast or brisket, trimmed
12-oz. can regular or non-alcoholic beer
10-1/2 oz. can French onion soup
10-1/2 oz. can beef broth
9 to 10 crusty rolls, split
softened butter to taste
granulated garlic to taste
Optional: sliced mozzarella cheese

Place beef in a large slow cooker; add beer, soup and broth. Cover and cook on low setting for 7 hours. Shortly before serving time, spread rolls with butter; sprinkle with garlic. Slice beef and place on the rolls. Top with cheese, if using. Wrap each sandwich in aluminum foil. Bake at 350 degrees for 10 minutes, or until heated through and cheese is melted. Serve with au jus sauce from slow cooker for dipping. Makes 9 to 10 servings.

Caramelized Onions

Claudia Keller
Carrollton, GA

If you like sautéed onions on sandwiches, you'll love this recipe that practically cooks itself. My husband can't get enough of them!

3 lbs. yellow onions, halved and thinly sliced
3 T. extra-virgin olive oil
1/2 t. salt

Place onions in a large slow cooker. Drizzle with olive oil; sprinkle with salt. Cover and cook on low setting for about 10 hours, until onions are soft and golden, stirring once or twice. Remove onions with a slotted spoon to covered containers. May be refrigerated for one week or frozen for 3 months. Makes about 3 cups.

Hot Tamale Spiced Cider

Tina Butler
Royse City, TX

Christmas isn't the same without a cup of this festive holiday cider! When I tasted it at a party, I was instantly hooked. Everyone can serve themselves as the cider stays warm and cozy in the slow cooker. Double this recipe for a crowd.

6 c. apple cider
1/4 c. chewy red cinnamon
   candies

1/4 t. whole cloves
1/8 t. nutmeg
Garnish: cinnamon sticks

Combine all ingredients except garnish in a slow cooker. Cover and cook on high setting for one hour, until hot and candies are melted. Strain cider through a wire sieve; discard cloves and the gummy part of the candies. Return cider to slow cooker; turn to low setting for serving. Serve hot in mugs, garnished with cinnamon stick stirrers. Makes 6 servings.

Add a bit of sparkle and spice to holiday drinks...tie a little ornament or bauble onto a cinnamon stick. The cinnamon stick is a great stirrer, while the ornament dangles over your mug of hot cocoa or mulled cider.

Festive Fuss-Free Party Food

Holiday Cider

Lisa Burns
Findlay, OH

This recipe is a tradition with my family every year when we gather for Christmas. It is so nice to sit down with a cup and enjoy all the family conversations. You can make this recipe in the morning and just leave it in the slow cooker set on low all day. It's such a comforting and relaxing beverage!

1 gal. apple cider
4 4-inch sticks cinnamon
1/2 c. brown sugar, packed

2 t. whole cloves
1/4 t. ground ginger
1 orange, unpeeled and sliced

Mix all ingredients in a large slow cooker. Cover and cook on low setting for 2 to 5 hours. Serves 12 to 15.

A simple greenery garland framed around a doorway can double as a Christmas card holder. Just use mini clothespins to clip holiday cards across the top and down each side.

Saucy Wieners & Meatballs

Susan Buetow
Du Quoin, IL

This is my most-requested hot dish every year at my Christmas open house. Each year I make more & more...I'm now up to using two large slow cookers for the event! My Auntie Shirley shared the recipe nearly 20 years ago when I was a young bride. I like to set out long fondue forks so guests can spear out their goodies.

1 lb. ground turkey
1/2 c. onion, finely chopped
10 crackers, finely crushed

18-oz. bottle barbecue sauce
12-oz. jar currant or grape jelly
14-oz. pkg. cocktail wieners

In a bowl, mix together turkey, onion and crackers. Form into quarter-size meatballs. Add meatballs to a slow cooker; top with barbecue sauce and jelly. Cover and cook on high setting for 4 hours. Add wieners; stir gently to coat with sauce. Cover and cook for one additional hour. Turn slow cooker to low setting for serving. Serve with toothpicks. Makes about 20 servings.

For a warm, cozy holiday fragrance, simmer cinnamon sticks, citrus peel, whole cloves and nutmeg in a mini slow cooker. Just add 2 to 3 cups of water and set on low.

Festive Fuss-Free Party Food

Gingered Chicken Wings

Cathy Hiller
Salt Lake City, UT

Great for game-day parties and busy-day family meals.
Pass the wings and pass the napkins!

3 lbs. chicken wings
2/3 c. soy sauce
4 green onions, chopped
4 cloves garlic, minced
2 T. honey

4 t. oil
2 t. ground ginger
Garnish: additional chopped
   green onions

Place wings in a slow cooker. Mix remaining ingredients in a small bowl; drizzle over wings. Cover and cook on low setting for 6 to 8 hours, until wings are glazed and chicken juices run clear when pierced. Garnish with more green onions. Serves 6 to 8.

Holiday Chutney

Megan Brooks
Antioch, TN

Delicious with roast pork, or for a delicious party snack, spoon chutney over a brick of cream cheese. Serve with crackers.

2 c. tart apples, peeled, cored
   and chopped
1/2 c. golden raisins
1/2 c. honey
3 T. cider vinegar

1/2 t. ground ginger
1/2 t. dry mustard
1/2 t. curry powder
1/4 t. salt

Combine apples and raisins in a mini slow cooker. Stir together remaining ingredients in a small bowl; pour over fruit mixture and stir. Cover and cook on low setting for 6 hours. Cool; spoon into a covered container. Makes about 2-1/2 cups.

For lots of sparkle, set a plump candle in a clear dish and
surround it with rock salt.

Richelle's Pulled Pork

Richelle Leck
Gananoque, Ontario

This tried & true recipe makes fantastic pulled pork to share with loved ones and friends...they keep coming back for more! The pork freezes nicely too.

1 t. oil
1 c. barbecue sauce
1/2 c. cider vinegar
1/2 c. chicken broth
1/4 c. brown sugar, packed
1/4 c. molasses
1 T. Worcestershire sauce
1 T. mustard

1 T. chili powder
1 t. cumin seed or dried thyme
1 t. instant coffee granules
1/2 t. cinnamon
1 onion, halved and sliced
2 cloves garlic, chopped
4-lb. pork shoulder roast
8 to 10 sandwich buns, split

Spread oil in the bottom of a large slow cooker. Add remaining ingredients and stir; place pork in slow cooker. Cover and cook on high setting for 5 to 6 hours, until pork is very tender. Remove pork to a plate. Shred, discarding any fat and bones. Return pork to mixture in slow cooker. Cover and cook on low setting for one to 2 more hours. To serve, scoop pork onto buns. Serves 8 to 10.

Add big red ribbon bows to stair railings, drawer handles, lamp bases and potted plants for a dash of Christmas color in a snap.

Festive Fuss-Free Party Food

Tasty Turkey Sloppy Joes

Lisa Ann Panzino-DiNunzio
Vineland, NJ

*A deliciously sloppy comfort food from my mom that's sure
to please. Although, with my dad's name being Joe, he would
love to see the name of this recipe changed!*

2 T. olive oil
2 lbs. lean ground turkey
1 onion, finely chopped
1 green pepper, diced
2 8-oz. cans tomato sauce

2 1.3-oz. pkgs. sloppy Joe
   seasoning mix
2 T. brown sugar, packed
1 c. water
10 sandwich buns, split

Heat oil in a large skillet over medium heat. Add turkey and cook until
no longer pink. Add onion and green pepper; cook 2 minutes longer.
Drain; transfer turkey mixture to a slow cooker. Stir in remaining
ingredients except buns. Cover and cook on low setting for 4 to
5 hours. To serve, spoon 1/2 cup of turkey mixture onto each bun.
Makes 10 servings.

Slow cookers come in so many sizes, you might want to have more
than one! A 4-quart size is handy for recipes that will feed about four people,
while a 5-1/2 to 6-quart one is just right for larger families and potlucks.
Just have room for one? Choose an oval slow cooker...roasts and
whole chickens will fit perfectly.

Hot Buttered Rum

Ellie Brandel
Milwaukie, OR

So welcoming for holiday entertaining...and your house will smell good too!

2 c. brown sugar, packed
1/2 c. butter, sliced
3 4-oz. sticks cinnamon
6 whole cloves
1/8 t. salt

1/2 t. nutmeg
2 qts. hot water
2 c. rum
Garnish: whipped cream,
    nutmeg to taste

Combine all ingredients except rum and garnish in a slow cooker. Stir well. Cover and cook on low setting for 5 hours. Add rum; stir to blend. Serve in mugs, garnished with a dollop of whipped cream and a dusting of nutmeg. Serves 10 to 12.

Set the mood with jolly Christmas music! Ask guest to bring along their favorites for a festive variety all evening long.

Calico Ham & Bean Soup

Diane Cohen
Breinigsville, PA

So good with warm buttered cornbread on a cold day!

1-1/2 c. dried mixed beans
3 c. chicken broth or water
2 c. cooked ham, cubed
14-1/2 oz. can diced tomatoes
1 c. carrots, peeled and chopped
1 c. onion, chopped

1 c. celery, chopped
1 t. dried basil
1 t. dried oregano
1/4 t. pepper
2 bay leaves
Optional: hot pepper sauce

Place beans in a large saucepan; add enough water to cover beans completely. Bring to a boil over medium-high heat. Reduce heat and simmer, uncovered, for 10 minutes. Drain beans; transfer to a slow cooker. Add broth or water, undrained tomatoes and remaining ingredients. Cover and cook on low setting for 8 to 10 hours, or on high setting for 4 to 5 hours. Discard bay leaves before serving. Serves 5.

Put together a savory soup in your slow cooker, then enjoy some winter fun with your family. After a snowy hike or ice skating, a hot, delicious dinner will be waiting for you...what could be cozier?

Come In & Warm Up!

Snow-Day Potato Soup

Susann Minall-Hunter
Spring Hill, FL

*My mom always had this soup ready for us when we had been
playing outside in the snow. Real stick-to-your-ribs soup!*

6 potatoes, peeled and diced
2 leeks, chopped
2 onions, chopped
1 carrot, peeled and thinly sliced
1 stalk celery, sliced
4 c. water
1/2 t. pepper

4 cubes chicken bouillon
2 10-3/4 oz. cans cream of
   mushroom soup
1 T. dried parsley
2 T. butter
12-oz. can evaporated milk
Garnish: chopped fresh chives

Combine all ingredients except evaporated milk and garnish in a large
slow cooker. Cover and cook on low setting for 8 to 10 hours, or on
high setting for 3 to 4 hours. Stir in milk during the last hour. Serve
garnished with chives. Makes 6 servings.

Stuffed Green Pepper Soup

Darlene Jones
Milford, MA

*A hearty, quick meal that everyone likes. I have even substituted
soy crumbles and vegetable bouillon for my vegetarian daughters.*

1 lb. extra-lean ground beef
1 c. onion, diced
14-1/2 oz. can diced tomatoes
2 c. green peppers, chopped
15-oz. can tomato sauce

3 c. water
1 T. beef bouillon granules
1/2 t. dried basil
1/2 t. dried oregano
1 c. cooked brown rice

In a skillet over medium heat, brown beef with onion. Drain; transfer
to a slow cooker. Add undrained tomatoes and remaining ingredients.
Cover and cook on low setting for 6 to 8 hours. Makes 8 servings.

Pull out your oversize coffee mugs when serving soup. They're just right for
sharing hearty servings, and the handles make them so easy to hold onto.

7-Can Chili Soup

Kathy Dunn
Niceville, FL

This is my most-requested soup from my family & friends. It is so easy and you can make it in just minutes. I have had grown men moan when they find that the crock is empty. Enjoy!

1 lb. ground beef
1 onion, diced
2 15-oz. cans chili with or
    without beans
15-1/4 oz. can corn
15-oz. can mixed vegetables
14-1/2 oz. can diced tomatoes

10-3/4 oz. can tomato soup
10-oz. can diced tomatoes with
    green chiles
2 c. water
Garnish: sour cream, shredded
    Cheddar cheese

In a skillet over medium heat, brown beef with onion. Drain; transfer to a slow cooker. Add all cans to slow cooker; do not drain. Stir in water. Cover and cook on low setting for 4 hours. Serve topped with sour cream and shredded cheese. Makes 10 to 12 servings.

For a thoughtful gift that's sure to be appreciated, purchase a calendar and fill in birthdays, anniversaries and other important family events... a nice gift for those new to the family!

Come In & Warm Up!

Ellen's Tortilla Soup

Sharon Buxton
Warsaw, OH

My sister gave me this super-easy recipe several years ago and I've been enjoying it ever since. I like to make it using leftover holiday turkey.

4 boneless, skinless chicken breasts, or 4 c. cooked turkey, cubed
2 10-oz. cans diced tomatoes and chiles with lime juice & cilantro
4-oz. can chopped green chiles
15-1/2 oz. can black beans, drained and rinsed
15-oz. can tomato sauce
1 c. salsa
Garnish: sour cream, shredded Cheddar cheese, tortilla chips

Place chicken or turkey in a large slow cooker. Add undrained tomatoes, undrained chiles, beans, tomato sauce and salsa. Cover and cook on low setting for about 8 hours. If using chicken breasts, during last 2 hours remove chicken and shred; return to crock. Serve individual bowls garnished with sour cream, cheese and tortilla chips. Makes 8 to 10 servings.

A soup supper menu doesn't need to be fussy, and the serving style is "help yourself!" A variety of soups kept warm in slow cookers, along with some rolls and a crock of creamery butter, is all that's needed. No kitchen duty at this gathering...just relax and enjoy each other's company.

Easy Chicken Corn Chowder

Jess Brunink
Whitehall, MI

This creamy chowder is a fave of the whole family! My family has dairy allergies, and it isn't easy to substitute for cream in soups and chowders without losing that creaminess, but creamed corn does the trick.

2 boneless, skinless chicken
    breasts, cooked and diced
3 14-3/4 oz. cans creamed corn
15-1/4 oz. can corn, drained

1 to 2 potatoes, peeled and diced
1 green pepper, diced
1 onion, diced
1 T. garlic, minced

Combine all ingredients in a slow cooker; stir gently. Cover and cook on low setting for 6 to 8 hours. Makes 6 servings.

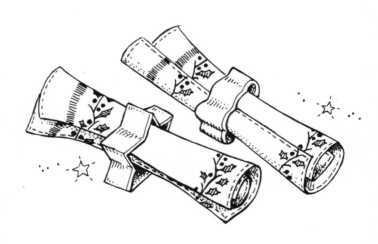

Cookie cutters make clever napkin rings...just slip the rolled-up napkin through the center. With a different shape for each person, it's always easy to know whose napkin is whose.

Come In & Warm Up!

Vegetarian Vegetable Soup

Barb Bargdill
Gooseberry Patch

*This hearty soup is so easy to get started in the morning before
I leave for work. Sometimes I'll add a cup of cooked soup
pasta stars or alphabets shortly before the soup is done.*

32-oz. bottle cocktail vegetable
   juice
2 16-oz. pkgs. frozen mixed
   soup vegetables
14-oz. can vegetable broth
3 c. water

6-oz. can tomato paste
1/2 c. onion, chopped
1 T. garlic, chopped
1/2 t. Italian seasoning
1 t. salt
1 t. sugar

Combine all ingredients in a large slow cooker; stir well. Cover and
cook on low setting for 6 to 8 hours. Makes 12 to 15 servings.

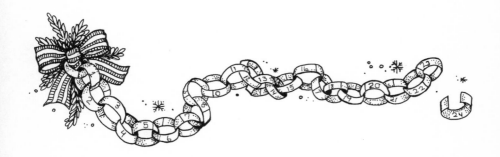

To little ones, it can seem sooo long 'til Santa Claus arrives! Have them
make a big chain of paper links and give each link a number from 1 to 25.
Every morning at breakfast, they can remove a link...and it's
one day closer to Christmas!

1-2-3 Chunky Turkey Soup

Melody Chencharick
Julian, PA

Need a way to use up some leftover turkey from the holidays? Toss it in the slow cooker and make some fantastic soup. If your family doesn't care for lima beans, use white kidney or black beans.

3 c. turkey or chicken broth
3/4 to 1 c. cooked turkey, cubed
1/2 c. frozen baby lima beans
1 potato, peeled and cubed
2 stalks celery, chopped

1/2 c. onion, chopped
1/3 c. carrot, peeled and sliced
1/2 c. spiral pasta, uncooked
1 T. fresh parsley, snipped
1 t. pepper

Combine all ingredients in a slow cooker; stir well. Cover and cook on low setting for 6 to 8 hours. Serves 4.

Share the Christmas spirit with a good deed...shovel the driveway and sidewalk for a neighbor. When you reach the doorstep, be sure to knock on the door and wish them a happy holiday! Back home, warm up with a hot bowl of soup from your slow cooker.

Come In & Warm Up!

Dilly Casserole Bread

Regina Wickline
Pebble Beach, CA

An old family favorite! You can't go wrong with this hearty,
savory bread...it really makes a soup supper special.

1/4 c. warm water
1 env. active dry yeast
1 c. cream-style cottage cheese,
  warmed
1 T. butter, softened
2 T. sugar
1 T. dried, minced onion

2 t. dill seed
1 t. salt
1/4 t. baking soda
1 egg, beaten
2-1/4 to 2-1/2 c. all-purpose
  flour

Heat water until very warm, about 110 to 115 degrees. Combine water
and yeast in a cup; let stand for 5 minutes. In a large bowl, combine
yeast mixture and remaining ingredients except flour. Add flour
gradually, beating well after each addition, until a stiff dough forms.
Turn dough into a greased and floured 1-1/2 quart casserole dish or a
32-ounce metal coffee can; place in slow cooker. Place 4 paper towels
on top of slow cooker to absorb condensation. Cover and cook on
high setting for 3 to 4 hours. Remove lid; let stand for 5 minutes.
Turn out bread; serve warm. Makes one loaf.

Tuck a loaf of freshly baked bread in a basket with some sweet
creamy butter, a jar of homemade soup and a farmhouse bowl.
A warm-hearted gift on a chilly winter's day!

Mandy's Best Beef Stew

Amanda Johnson
Marysville, OH

This recipe is fantastic in the slow cooker! Serve with warm crusty bread.

1/2 c. all-purpose flour
salt and pepper to taste
1 lb. stew beef cubes
1 to 2 T. oil
4 potatoes, peeled and cubed
4 carrots, peeled and chopped

2 stalks celery, chopped
1/4 c. dried, chopped onion
2 cubes beef bouillon
2 bay leaves
dried parsley to taste

Combine flour and seasonings in a shallow bowl; dredge beef cubes until coated. Heat oil in a skillet over medium-high heat; add beef and brown on all sides. Transfer beef to a slow cooker; add remaining ingredients and enough water to half-cover all ingredients. Cover and cook on low setting for 8 to 10 hours, or high setting for 4 to 5 hours, until beef is tender. Discard bay leaves before serving. Makes 4 servings.

For the sweetest family times, snuggle under a cozy throw and read favorite Christmas story books together. Young children will love being read to, while older kids may enjoy taking turns reading aloud from "The Night Before Christmas" or "A Christmas Carol."

Come In & Warm Up!

French Onion Soup

Kristen Taylor
Fort Smith, AR

*It's so nice to come home to the delicious aroma of this soup
ready and waiting in the slow cooker! The adults in
our family especially enjoy it.*

1/4 c. butter, sliced	3 32-oz. containers beef broth
1/4 c. olive oil	1 c. red wine or beef broth
4 sweet onions, thinly sliced	8 to 10 slices baguette or
1/4 c. all-purpose flour	French bread
salt and pepper to taste	8 to 10 slices baby Swiss cheese

Melt butter with olive oil in a large skillet over medium heat. Add
onions; cover and cook until onions are soft and translucent. Sprinkle
with flour; cook and stir until onions are golden. Season with salt and
pepper. Spoon onions into a large slow cooker. Add broth and wine or
broth. Cover and cook on low setting for 7 to 8 hours. Shortly before
serving time, arrange bread slices on a baking sheet. Top with cheese
slices; broil until bread is toasted and cheese is melted. Ladle soup into
bowls; top each with a toasted bread slice. Makes 8 to 10 servings.

What's more cozy than gathering 'round the fireplace for hot cocoa and
a chat? Stencil pine trees and stars on a large galvanized tub to fill with logs.
Set by the fire to save trips out into the blustery evening for firewood.

Ham & Lentil Stew

Patricia Flak
Erie, PA

A great way to use some of that leftover Christmas ham...
it has lots of healthy ingredients too!

1 c. cooked ham, diced
2-1/4 c. chicken broth
4 c. water
2 c. dried lentils, uncooked
2 c. carrots, peeled and diced
2 c. celery, sliced

1 c. onion, diced
1 T. garlic, minced
1 t. dried oregano
1/4 t. pepper
6-oz. pkg. fresh baby spinach
2 T. lemon juice

In a large slow cooker, combine all ingredients except spinach and lemon juice. Cover and cook on low setting for 7 hours, or until lentils are tender. Stir in spinach. Cover and cook 5 minutes more, or until spinach is wilted. Stir in lemon juice and serve. Makes 8 servings.

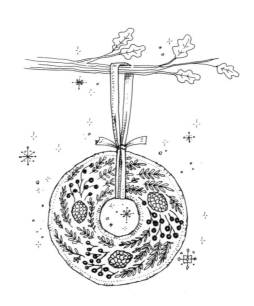

For a magical ice wreath, arrange cranberries and pine trimmings in
a ring mold and fill with water. Freeze until solid, then pop out of the mold.
Hang outdoors from a tree branch with a sturdy ribbon.

Come In & Warm Up!

Best Cabbage Soup

Rebecca Wright
Tulsa, OK

On a cold winter's day, this soup will warm you to the bottom of your toes! It's simple to fix and my kids love it. Serve with brown & serve rolls.

16-oz. pkg. smoked pork
   sausage, cut into
   1-inch pieces
28-oz. can diced tomatoes
1/2 head cabbage, thinly sliced
2 carrots, peeled and chopped

2 stalks celery, chopped
2 potatoes, peeled and chopped
2 14-1/2 oz. cans chicken broth
20-oz. can vegetable cocktail
   juice

In a large slow cooker, combine sausage, undrained tomatoes and vegetables. Add broth and juice. Cover and cook on low setting for 6 to 8 hours, or on high setting for 3 hours, until vegetables are tender. Makes 6 servings.

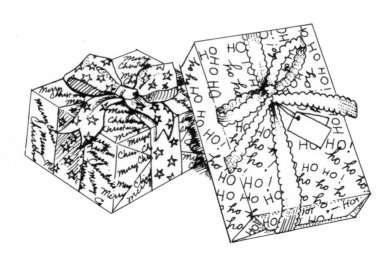

Turn ho-hum plain kraft paper into ho-ho-ho with holiday rubber stamps and a red or green ink pad...easy enough for a child to do!

Jammin' Beef Stew

Glenna Kennedy
Collingwood, Ontario

*I found this recipe many years ago and thought I'd give it a try.
I have been making it ever since. I usually serve this with
fresh-baked tea biscuits.*

2 lbs. stew beef cubes
1/4 c. all-purpose flour
1-1/2 t. salt
1/4 t. pepper
14-1/2 oz. can beef broth
6 new potatoes, quartered
1 c. onion, chopped

3 carrots, peeled and thickly
  sliced on the diagonal
14-1/2 oz. can diced tomatoes
1/2 c. grape jam or jelly
1 T. Worcestershire sauce
2 T. fresh parsley, chopped

Place beef in a slow cooker coated with non-stick vegetable spray.
Combine flour, salt and pepper in a cup; sprinkle over beef and toss to
coat. Add remaining ingredients except parsley; stir. Cover and cook
on low setting for 8 to 10 hours, or on high setting for 5 to 6 hours.
Stir in parsley and additional salt and pepper, if desired. Serves 4.

Browning isn't required for slow-cooker beef stew, but it does add lots
of flavor. For best results, pat the stew cubes dry with a paper towel
before browning. Don't crowd the pieces in the pan, and be sure to
stir up all the tasty browned bits at the bottom.

Come In & Warm Up!

Easy Beef Stew

Rogene Rogers
Bemidji, MN

This is my favorite recipe for beef stew.

1 lb. stew beef cubes
2 T. all-purpose flour
2 T. oil
2-1/4 c. potatoes, peeled
    and cubed
1 c. carrots, peeled and sliced

1-1/2 c. celery, sliced
1/2 c. onion, chopped
2 t. beef bouillon granules
3-1/2 c. low-sodium cocktail
    vegetable juice

In a bowl, coat beef with flour. Heat oil in a large skillet over medium-high heat; brown beef on all sides. Place vegetables in a slow cooker; top with beef. Stir bouillon into vegetable juice; pour juice over beef. Cover and cook on low setting for 9 to 10 hours. Makes 6 to 8 servings.

Fresh-Baked Dinner Rolls

Virginia Watson
Scranton, PA

So handy when the oven is already in use.

8 to 10 frozen dinner rolls

Garnish: softened butter

Line the bottom of a large slow cooker with a circle of parchment paper. Lightly spray with non-stick vegetable spray. Arrange frozen rolls in slow cooker. Cover and cook on low setting for about 1-1/4 hours, until rolls have thawed and risen. Turn slow cooker to high setting. Cover and cook for 1-1/4 hours, until set. For a more golden finish, remove rolls to a baking sheet; broil for 90 seconds, or until golden. Brush baked rolls with butter. Makes 8 to 10 rolls.

Herb butter is so versatile! Blend 1/2 cup softened butter and a teaspoon each of chopped fresh parsley, chives and dill. Form butter into a log on a piece of plastic wrap and freeze, or pack into a crock for a handy hostess gift.

Chicken & Quinoa Chili

Lori Rosenberg
University Heights, OH

This chili has a great texture that's just a little bit different. If the chili absorbs too much liquid, just add more broth. I serve it with avocado salsa to balance the heat of the chili.

2 boneless, skinless chicken breasts
28-oz. can diced tomatoes
14-1/2 oz. can diced tomatoes with chiles
15-1/2 oz. can chili beans, drained and rinsed
15-1/2 oz. can black beans, drained and rinsed
15-1/4 oz. can corn, drained
2 c. chicken broth
1 c. quinoa, uncooked and rinsed
2 to 3 t. chili powder
2 t. garlic powder
2 t. ground cumin
1/2 t. red pepper flakes
Garnish: chopped avocado salsa, other toppings

Place chicken in a large slow cooker. Add undrained tomatoes and remaining ingredients except garnish; stir gently. Cover and cook on low setting for 6 to 8 hours, or on high setting for 4 to 6 hours. Remove chicken and shred with 2 forks; return to slow cooker. Serve chili garnished as desired. Makes 8 servings.

Freeze chili in small containers...later, pop in the microwave for chili dogs, nachos or baked potatoes at a moment's notice. A terrific time-saver during the busy holiday season.

Come In & Warm Up!

Annette's Chili Soup

Annette Ceravolo
Hoover, AL

This soup has been made by family & friends over the years. Each person has added something to it...this is my version. It's spicy and so good. Serve with biscuits or cornbread.

1 lb. lean ground beef
1 onion, finely chopped
3 to 4 15-1/2 oz. cans kidney
    beans
10-oz. can diced tomatoes
    with chiles

1/2 c. dry red wine or beef broth
4 t. chili powder
1/2 t. garlic, minced
salt and pepper to taste

In a skillet over medium heat, brown beef and onion together; drain well. Combine beef mixture, undrained beans, undrained tomatoes and remaining ingredients in a large slow cooker. Cover and cook on high setting for 3 to 4 hours. Serves 4.

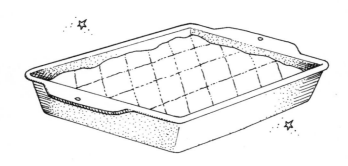

If you like sweet cornbread, you'll love this simple recipe! Mix together an 8-1/2 ounce corn muffin mix, a 9-ounce yellow cake mix, 1/2 cup water, 1/3 cup milk and 2 beaten eggs. Pour into a greased slow cooker. Cover and cook on high setting for 2 hours, or until set in the center.

Cozy Cabin Stew

Maegan Stauffer
Findlay, OH

*I tossed this stew together one snowy day while raiding my freezer.
It filled our home with a wonderful aroma...it was an instant hit with
my husband and my daughter! I chose the name because we love to
dream of being in a cozy cabin on cold Ohio days.*

3 to 4 russet potatoes, peeled
   and chopped
15 to 20 frozen meatballs
1 green pepper, chopped
1 onion, chopped

2 c. water
Worcestershire sauce to taste
garlic salt and pepper to taste
Garnish: shredded Italian-blend
   cheese

Layer potatoes, meatballs, green pepper and onion in a large slow
cooker; add water. Sprinkle generously with Worcestershire sauce,
salt and pepper. Cover and cook on high setting for 4 hours. Turn slow
cooker to low setting; cook for one more hour. Sprinkle with cheese
at serving time. Serves 4 to 6.

Taco Soup

Sara Sagerer
San Diego, CA

*As my hubby says, I can cook this with my eyes closed! Even my
teenagers can make this and it fills them up too. It is great for
cold winter nights or for a potluck dish in a pinch.*

1 lb. ground beef or turkey
3 15-1/2 oz. cans kidney beans
   and/or other beans
2 1-1/4 oz. pkgs. mild or spicy
   taco seasoning mix

14-1/2 oz. can beef broth
Garnish: sour cream, shredded
   Cheddar cheese, diced onion,
   snipped fresh cilantro,
   tortilla chips

Brown meat in a skillet over medium heat; drain and add to a slow
cooker. Add undrained beans, seasoning mix and broth; stir to
combine. Cover and cook on low setting for 6 to 8 hours. Serve soup
garnished with desired toppings. Makes 6 to 8 servings.

Come In & Warm Up!

BBQ Brunswick Stew

Stephanie Westfall
Dallas, GA

My husband and son love this slow-cooker recipe. It's a cinch to make and very good on a cold winter night.

2 10-oz. cans beef in
   barbecue sauce
12-1/2 oz. can white chicken,
   drained and flaked
2 14-1/2 oz. cans diced
   tomatoes

15-1/4 oz. can corn
14-3/4 oz. can creamed corn
14-1/2 oz. can lima beans

Combine beef, chicken and undrained vegetables in a slow cooker. Cover and cook on low setting for 2 to 3 hours, until hot and bubbly. Makes 6 servings.

Pantry Tomato Soup

Christina Sheppard
Centerville, OH

I was craving a good, homemade tomato soup, and I had lots of different ingredients in my pantry, so I put them all together and came up with this. It's delicious!

14-1/2 oz. can diced tomatoes
   with basil, garlic and
   oregano
28-oz. can tomato sauce
14-1/2 oz. can tomato soup

14-1/2 oz. can chicken broth
Garnish: sour cream, grated
   Parmesan cheese, fish-
   shaped crackers

Combine undrained tomatoes, sauce, soup and broth in a slow cooker. Cover and cook on low setting for 2 hours, or until heated through. Garnish as desired. Makes 6 to 8 servings.

Remember the birds at Christmas time. Decorate an outdoor tree with birdseed bells, suet balls, garlands of fruit and hollowed-out orange halves filled with birdseed.

Honeyed Whole-Wheat Bread

Melanie Lowe
Dover, DE

*Fun to make with the kids...and there's nothing better than
a slice of warm buttered homemade bread!*

3 c. whole-wheat flour, divided
1 c. all-purpose flour, divided
2 c. warm milk, about 110 to
   115 degrees

1/4 c. honey
2 T. oil
1 env. active dry yeast
3/4 t. salt

In a large bowl, combine 1-1/2 cups whole-wheat flour, 1/2 cup
all-purpose flour, milk, honey, oil, yeast and salt. Beat with an electric
mixer on medium speed for 2 minutes. Beat or stir in remaining whole-
wheat flour; add remaining all-purpose flour until dough is no longer
sticky. Place dough in a greased one-quart casserole dish; set dish in
slow cooker. Cover and cook on high setting for 3 hours, or until edges
of bread are golden. Remove dish from slow cooker to a wire rack; let
stand 5 minutes. Turn bread out onto wire rack; cool. Makes one loaf.

A loaf of homemade bread is always a welcome gift! Make sure it
stays fresh and tasty...let the bread cool completely before wrapping
well in plastic wrap or aluminum foil.

Come In & Warm Up!

Crock o' Healthy Beer Bread

Erin Brock
Charleston, WV

Serve up thick slices...delicious with a bowl of hot soup!

1-1/2 c. all-purpose flour
1-1/4 c. whole-wheat flour
2 T. wheat germ
2 T. ground flax seed
1 T. baking powder

1 T. sugar
1 t. salt
14-oz. can regular or
   non-alcoholic beer

Grease a 4-quart slow cooker well; turn to high setting. In a large bowl, combine all ingredients; stir together until a sticky dough forms. Form dough into a loaf; press evenly into slow cooker. Cover and cook on high setting for 3 hours. Turn out bread; cool on a wire rack. Makes one loaf.

Cinnamon Apple Butter

Kris Kellis
Salisbury, NC

A good friend shared this recipe with me years ago. I love to make it in the fall for Christmas gift giving. Very easy and very popular!

5-1/2 lbs. apples, peeled, cored
   and sliced
4 c. sugar
2 to 3 t. cinnamon

1/4 t. ground cloves
1/4 t. nutmeg
1/4 t. salt

Combine all ingredients in a large slow cooker. Cook, uncovered, on high setting for one hour. Turn to low setting. Cover and cook for 9 to 11 hours, stirring occasionally, until thick and dark brown. Uncover and cook for one additional hour, until thickened. Cool. Spoon into freezer containers or sterilized jars. Cover and refrigerate for up to 3 weeks, or freeze for up to 3 months. Makes about 10 pints.

Wedding Soup

Barbara Topp
Sparta, NJ

This is a family favorite, great on a snowy day

16-oz. pkg. frozen meatballs
2 chicken breasts, cooked and
    shredded
2 stalks celery, sliced
1 carrot, peeled and sliced
1/2 c. grated Parmesan or
    Romano cheese

6 c. chicken broth
2 t. salt-free herb seasoning
1 to 2 t. garlic, minced
2 c. fresh spinach, chopped
1/4 c. small soup pasta or
    long-cooking rice, uncooked

In a large slow cooker, combine all ingredients except spinach and pasta or rice. Cover and cook on low setting for 6 to 8 hours. Stir in spinach and pasta or rice during the last hour of cooking. Makes 6 to 8 servings.

Start a tradition of filling the children's stockings with old-fashioned small gifts like penny candy, wooden puzzles, tiny toys and a juicy piece of ripe fruit. You may be surprised at how eagerly these surprises will be anticipated!

Come In & Warm Up!

Merry Minestrone

Lynnette Jones
East Flat Rock, NC

It's so easy to fill up your slow cooker with this hearty soup on busy holiday days, whether you're going shopping or baking cookies at home. I like to serve it with cheese bread and a green salad.

19-oz. can minestrone soup
14-1/2 oz. can stewed tomatoes
16-oz. can pinto beans, drained
16-oz. can kidney beans,
   drained
11-oz. can corn, drained

8-oz. can tomato sauce
4-oz. can diced green chiles
1/2 t. garlic powder
1/2 t. onion salt
Optional: 1/2 lb. browned
   ground beef

Combine soup, undrained tomatoes and remaining ingredients in a slow cooker. Cover and cook on low setting for 4 to 6 hours. Makes 6 to 8 servings.

Stock your freezer with comforting home-cooked soups and stews, ready to enjoy anytime! They freeze well for up to 3 months in plastic freezer containers...just thaw overnight in the refrigerator and add a little water when reheating.

Hearty Pumpkin Chili

Claire Bertram
Lexington, KY

*My family was bored with the same old ground beef & bean chili,
so I gave this recipe a try. It really hits the spot! It's easily to double
when the kids will be bringing their friends home for supper.*

1 T. oil
1 lb. ground turkey
1 c. onion, chopped
1 c. green and/or yellow
    pepper, diced
1 clove garlic, minced
14-1/2 oz. can diced tomatoes

15-oz. can pumpkin
1-1/2 T. chili powder
1/2 t. pepper
1/8 t. salt
Garnish: shredded Cheddar
    cheese, sour cream

Heat oil in a skillet over medium heat. Add turkey, onion, green and/or
yellow pepper and garlic; cook until turkey is browned and vegetables
are tender. Spoon turkey mixture into a slow cooker. Stir in undrained
tomatoes, pumpkin and seasonings. Cover and cook on low setting for
4 to 5 hours. Garnish individual servings with cheese and sour cream.
Makes 4 to 6 servings.

Dress up a stack of plain white gift bags with pom-pom snowman faces
and fabric scrap scarves. A hot glue gun pulls it all together in just a
few minutes. Tuck in tissue paper and gifts...now, aren't you clever!

Come In & Warm Up!

Chicken Taco Stew

Nikki Booth
Kinderhook, IL

Colorful and delicious, this hearty stew is perfect when everyone is coming in from sledding or ice skating.

14-1/2 oz. can diced tomatoes
15-1/2 oz. can black beans, drained and rinsed
15-1/2 oz. can kidney beans, drained and rinsed
14-3/4 oz. can corn, drained
1 onion, chopped

1 c. water
1-1/4 oz. pkg. taco seasoning mix
2 boneless, skinless chicken breasts
Garnish: shredded Cheddar cheese, tortilla chips

In a slow cooker, stir together undrained tomatoes and remaining ingredients except chicken and garnish. Lay chicken on top. Cover and cook on low setting for 6 to 8 hours, or on high setting for 3 to 4 hours. Shortly before serving, remove chicken; shred with 2 forks and return to slow cooker. Serve portions garnished with cheese and tortilla chips. Makes 4 to 6 servings.

Need to feed a few extra guests? It's easy to stretch a slow cooker full of soup. Some quick add-ins are canned beans, orzo pasta, ramen noodles and instant rice. Add cooked ingredients to slow cooker, and simmer for just a few minutes until heated through.

Hearty Fish Chowder

Marlene Campbell
Millinocket, ME

My husband and I enjoy this satisfying chowder for our
Christmas Eve dinner. Sometimes I add other seafood like
shrimp or crab in place of some of the haddock.

1 onion, chopped
1 carrot, peeled and sliced
2 stalks celery, sliced
1/4 c. water
2 lbs. haddock, thawed if frozen

10-3/4 oz. can cream of
  shrimp soup
1/4 c. milk
1/4 t. dried thyme
1/4 t. pepper

Combine onion, carrot and celery in a slow cooker. Add water; cover
and cook on high setting for 2 hours. Cut fish into large pieces, about
3 inches square. Place fish pieces on top of vegetables. Combine
remaining ingredients in a bowl; pour over fish. Reduce heat to low.
Cover and cook for 3-3/4 hours, or until fish flakes easily. Uncover;
break fish into smaller pieces with a fork and stir. Cover; turn off slow
cooker and let stand for 15 minutes before serving. Serves 4.

Christmas is here, merry old Christmas,
gift-bearing, heart-touching, joy-bringing Christmas,
day of grand memories, king of the year!
— Washington Irving

Come In & Warm Up!

Cream of Crab Soup

Bernice Hamburg
Baltimore, MD

This is a quick yet special recipe...we hope you enjoy it!

4 10-3/4 oz. cans cream of
   celery soup
1 lb. refrigerated lump or
   special crabmeat

1 qt. half-and-half
2 T. butter, sliced
2 T. seafood seasoning
Optional: milk

Combine all ingredients except milk in a large slow cooker; stir. Cover and cook on high setting for 4 to 6 hours, stirring frequently to prevent sticking. Soup will start out thin, but will thicken as it sets; stir in some milk if too thick. Serves 8 to 12.

Clam Chowder

Jewel Sharpe
Raleigh, NC

A tried & true recipe I like to use in cool weather when we go camping. So simple...so delicious!

3 10-3/4 oz. cans cream of
   potato soup
2 10-3/4 oz. cans New England
   clam chowder
1 pt. half-and-half

2 6/1-2 oz. cans chopped clams
1/2 c. onion, diced
1/2 c. butter, sliced
Garnish: saltine crackers

Combine all ingredients except crackers in a slow cooker. Cover and cook on low setting for 2 to 4 hours. Serve with crackers. Makes 6 to 8 servings.

Volunteer for a day at a local soup kitchen.
Whether you're chopping veggies, stirring the
kettle or serving up bowls of hot soup,
your help is sure to be appreciated.

Butternut Bisque

JoAnn

*Serve cups of this smooth bisque, dolloped with sour cream,
as a starter for holiday dinners.*

2 T. butter
1/2 c. onion, chopped
1 butternut squash, peeled
   and cubed
2 c. chicken broth

1/2 t. dried marjoram
1/4 t. pepper
1/8 t. cayenne pepper
8-oz. pkg. cream cheese, cubed

Melt butter in a skillet over medium heat; cook onion until almost tender. Spoon onion mixture into a slow cooker; add remaining ingredients except cream cheese. Cover and cook on low setting for 6 to 8 hours, until squash is tender. Working in batches, ladle squash mixture into a blender or food processor; cover and purée until smooth. Return puréed mixture to slow cooker; stir in cream cheese. Cover and cook on low setting for another 30 minutes, or until cheese is melted. Whisk until smooth. Makes 6 servings.

When cooking for Christmas, make good use of your freezer. You can prepare soups weeks in advance and freeze them until you are ready to serve them, garnished with a swirl of fresh cream. They're an elegant yet simple appetizer for your holiday meal.

Come In & Warm Up!

Cranberry-Orange Loaf

Dale Duncan
Cunningham, IA

*Oranges and cranberries just seem to go with the holidays!
Sometimes I'll drizzle it with powdered sugar icing. This bread
is delicious with a cup of spiced tea.*

3 c. all-purpose flour, divided
1-1/3 c. sugar
1 T. baking powder
1/4 t. baking soda
1/4 t. salt
2 c. hot water

2/3 c. powdered dry milk
1 egg, beaten
1/4 c. oil
1 c. sweetened dried cranberries,
chopped
2 t. orange zest

In a large bowl, mix together 2 cups flour, sugar, baking powder,
baking soda and salt; set aside. In a separate bowl, whisk together hot
water and milk; add to flour mixture along with egg and oil. Beat with
an electric mixer on medium speed for 2 minutes. Add remaining flour
and beat on low speed until well mixed. Fold in cranberries and orange
zest with a spoon; set aside. Line the bottom of a 4-quart slow cooker
with a circle of parchment paper; spray with non-stick vegetable spray.
Pour batter into slow cooker. Place 4 paper towels on top of slow
cooker to absorb condensation. Cover and cook on high setting for
2 to 3 hours, until firm on top, checking for doneness after 2 hours.
Bread will not be browned. Let stand for 10 minutes; turn out onto a
wire rack to cool. Makes one loaf.

Turn your holiday cards into a Christmas garland...a great party decoration!
Use mini clothespins to clip cards to a length of ribbon or twine. Add some
favorite holiday photos and handmade gift tags to create a heartfelt
display that family & friends are sure to enjoy.

Hearty Chicken Noodle Soup

Elizabeth Watts
Nowata, OK

Chopping and dicing the veggies for this recipe really helps me wind down after a long day. I like to let the soup cook overnight and get up early the the next morning to add the noodles. The house smells wonderful while it's cooking, and the soup is delicious.

2 boneless, skinless chicken
    breasts
32-oz. container chicken broth
3 c. water, divided
1 c. celery, chopped
3 carrots, peeled and thinly
    sliced
2 T. fresh parsley, chopped
1 bay leaf

1/2 t. dried thyme
1/2 t. garlic powder
1/4 t. poultry seasoning
1 t. salt
1/4 t. pepper
2 10-3/4 oz. cans cream of
    chicken soup
3 c. wide egg noodles, uncooked

Put chicken in a large slow cooker; pour in broth and 2 cups water. Add vegetables and seasonings; stir. Mix chicken soup and remaining water in a bowl; stir into mixture in slow cooker. Cover and cook on low setting for 6 to 8 hours, until chicken is tender. Discard bay leaf. Remove chicken and shred with 2 forks; return chicken to cooker. Stir in uncooked noodles. Cover and cook for one hour longer. Let stand for 10 minutes before serving.

Soup to go! Tuck a big jar of Hearty Chicken Noodle Soup, a packet of saltines and a cheery soup bowl into a basket. Sure to be equally appreciated by a friend with the sniffles or who simply doesn't get enough homemade meals!

Come In & Warm Up!

Lemon Tea Bread

Carrie O'Shea
Marina Del Rey, CA

A tender tart-sweet loaf that's perfect almost anytime.

2 c. all-purpose flour	2 eggs
1-1/2 t. baking powder	1/3 c. milk
1/4 t. salt	1/2 c. chopped walnuts
1/2 c. butter, softened	2 t. lemon zest
1 c. sugar	

In a bowl, stir together flour, baking powder and salt; set aside. In a separate large bowl, beat butter and sugar with an electric mixer on low speed until blended. Add eggs, one at a time; beat until fluffy. Beat in flour mixture alternately with milk, just until blended. Stir in nuts and lemon zest with a spoon. Pour batter into a greased and floured 32-ounce metal coffee can; place in slow cooker. Place 4 paper towels on top of slow cooker to absorb condensation. Cover and cook on high setting for 2 to 3 hours, until bread tests done with a wooden toothpick. Turn out bread onto a wire rack to cool for 10 minutes. Pierce bread with a fork; drizzle with Lemon Glaze. Serve warm. Makes one loaf.

Lemon Glaze:

1/4 c. lemon juice	1/3 c. sugar

Combine lemon juice and sugar in a saucepan. Cook and stir over medium heat until syrupy, about one minute.

Need a gift in a jiffy for a teacher, a neighbor or a friend with a new baby? Give a loaf of freshly baked quick bread wrapped in a pretty tea towel... it's sure to be appreciated.

Ultimate Bean Stew

Daniela Domin
Hazelton, PA

*I created this recipe hoping that my picky three-year-old twin
daughters would eat it. Now it's the only stew they will eat!*

16-oz. pkg. dried 16-bean
    soup mix
14-1/2 oz. can diced tomatoes
1 lb. boneless, skinless chicken,
    cubed

1 c. frozen corn
1 onion, chopped
2 14-1/2 oz. cans chicken broth
salt and pepper to taste

Cover beans with water; soak overnight. In the morning, drain beans.
Add beans, undrained tomatoes and remaining ingredients except salt
and pepper to a slow cooker. Cover and cook on low setting for 6 to
8 hours, or on high setting for 4 to 5 hours, until beans are tender.
Season with salt and pepper. Makes 6 to 8 servings.

Mixed Bean Soup

Blanche DeLay
Kamiah, ID

*My family always asks for my bean soup when the weather starts
getting cooler. Now & then I put a hot pepper in it to add
a little zip. Enjoy with homemade cornbread.*

1/2 c. dried navy beans
1/2 c. dried red beans
1/2 c. dried pinto beans
1 ham hock or 2 slices bacon

6 c. water
1/2 t. salt
1/4 t. pepper

Cover beans with water; soak overnight. In the morning, drain beans
and place in a slow cooker; add remaining ingredients. Cover and cook
on low setting for 8 to 9 hours, until beans are tender. At serving time,
remove ham hock, if using; dice meat and return to soup. Season with
more salt if desired. Makes 8 servings.

A quick & easy way to thicken bean soup...purée a cup of soup in a blender
or even mash it in a bowl, then stir it back into the soup pot.

Come In & Warm Up!

Turnip Greens & Beans Soup

Edra Zittauer
Guyton, GA

We have made this down-home soup in the slow cooker at work and shared with co-workers at lunchtime. Pass the cornbread!

3 15-1/2 oz. cans navy or Great
   Northern beans
2 14-1/2 oz. cans chicken broth
14-1/2 oz. can seasoned turnip
   greens
1 lb. smoked pork sausage,
   sliced 1/4-inch thick

onion salt, garlic salt and pepper
   to taste
1/3 c. instant mashed potato
   flakes

Combine all ingredients except potato flakes in a slow cooker; do not drain vegetables. Cover and cook on high setting for 3 to 4 hours. Stir in potato flakes; cover and cook an additional 10 to 15 minutes, until thickened. Serves 8.

Tie ornaments onto the Christmas tree with narrow strips
of homespun fabric...sweet and simple!

Corn & Sausage Chowder

Jill Ball
Highland, UT

Life is really busy at our house! If my family is going to eat a home-cooked meal, it needs to be easy...that's why we love this recipe. It is wonderful on cold winter nights. I can start it cooking in the morning before school and work, and have dinner ready when we all get home.

1 lb. smoked turkey sausage
3 c. frozen diced potatoes with
    onions and pepper
2 carrots, peeled and chopped
14-3/4 oz. can creamed corn

10-3/4 oz. can cream of
    mushroom soup
2 c. water
1/2 t. dried thyme
1/8 t. pepper

Brown sausage in a skillet over medium-high heat. Cut sausage into chunks and place in a slow cooker; top with potatoes and carrots. Combine remaining ingredients in a bowl; spoon into slow cooker. Cover and cook on low setting for 8 to 10 hours. Serves 6.

Soups and chowders are extra hearty served in bread bowls. Cut the tops off round crusty loaves and scoop out the soft bread inside. Brush with olive oil. Bake at 350 degrees for a few minutes until toasty, then ladle in soup.

Come In & Warm Up!

Chicken-Corn Soup

Nichole Sullivan
Santa Fe, TX

What better to eat on a cold day than a bowl of hot soup? I took some over to our Meemaw and she called later that evening to tell me, "Don't lose that recipe!" Try it yourself...you'll agree it's a keeper.

2 to 3 potatoes, peeled and diced
3 carrots, peeled and diced
2 stalks celery, diced
1/2 onion, diced
1 T. garlic, minced
1 to 2 lbs. boneless, skinless
    chicken breasts, diced
1 to 2 t. Italian seasoning
salt and pepper to taste
14-3/4 oz. can creamed corn
14-1/4 oz. can corn, drained
6-oz. can tomato paste
3 c. chicken broth
1/4 c. fresh cilantro, chopped

In a large slow cooker, layer potatoes, carrots, celery, onion and garlic. Add chicken, seasonings, both cans of corn and tomato paste. Top with broth and cilantro. Cover and cook on low setting for 8 to 9 hours, or on high setting for 4 to 5 hours. Makes 8 to 10 servings.

Take along a thermos of creamy hot soup on
an afternoon of holiday errands...it's sure
to give you a much-needed lift.

Cream of Broccoli Soup

Gloria Huff
Sandy Hook, VA

This is our favorite Sunday lunch. As a church minister of music, I am usually first to arrive at church and last to leave. A friend at a previous church gave me this recipe, and it's a winter must in our house! I have shared this recipe often.

10-oz. pkg. frozen chopped
    broccoli
1 onion, chopped
1/2 c. water
12-oz. can evaporated milk
10-3/4 oz. can cream of
    mushroom soup

10-3/4 oz. can cream of
    celery soup
10-3/4 oz. can cream of
    chicken soup
salt and pepper to taste
Garnish: favorite shredded
    cheese

In a saucepan over medium-high heat, cook broccoli and onion in water until onion is translucent. Do not drain. Transfer broccoli mixture to a slow cooker; stir in evaporated milk, soups, salt and pepper. Cover and cook on low setting for 3 to 4 hours. Add desired amount of cheese before serving. Serves 6 to 8.

Quickly turn a group of mismatched tag-sale candleholders into a shimmering set...spray them all with your favorite color of craft paint. All white or ivory looks snowy tucked among evergreen and holiday decorations...bright red or shiny gold is festive too.

Come In & Warm Up!

Boston Brown Bread

Kendall Hale
Lynn, MA

Serve with softened cream cheese...yummy!

1 c. rye flour
1 c. whole-wheat flour
1 c. cornmeal
1-1/2 t. baking soda
1 t. salt

3/4 c. molasses
2 c. buttermilk
Optional: 1 c. raisins
2 c. hot water

In a large bowl, combine flours, cornmeal, baking soda and salt. In a separate bowl, stir molasses into buttermilk. Stir molasses mixture gradually into flour mixture, just until moistened. Add raisins, if using. Spoon batter into 2 greased and floured 16-ounce metal cans; place in slow cooker. Cover tops of cans with aluminum foil. Place cans on a wire rack in a large slow cooker; carefully pour hot water around cans. Cover and cook on high setting for 2-1/2 to 3 hours. Remove cans and let stand 5 to 10 minutes. Remove ends of cans with a can opener; push bread out onto a wire rack. Cool. Makes 2 mini loaves.

For a simple winter centerpiece, arrange mini figurines on a cake stand, dust with glittery mica snow, then add the clear glass cover...charming!

Loaded Potato Soup

Sherry Webb
Ridgeway, VA

This potato soup is so rich, creamy and filling that it puts other potato soups to shame. All of my co-workers love it and can't wait for soup weather for me to make it...luckily it feeds a crowd!

5 lbs. potatoes, peeled, diced and cooked
2 14-1/2 oz. cans chicken broth
12-oz. can evaporated milk
8-oz. container sour cream
1/2 c. butter, sliced
2 T. salt-free herb seasoning

16-oz. pkg. shredded Cheddar cheese
16-oz. pkg. shredded Pepper Jack cheese
4 to 6 green onions, chopped
3-oz. pkg. bacon bits
saltine crackers

Place potatoes in a 7-quart slow cooker. Add broth, evaporated milk, sour cream, butter, seasoning and cheeses; stir well. Cover and cook on low setting for 4 hours, stirring occasionally. Add onions. Cover and continue cooking for one hour. Serve topped with bacon bits and crackers. Serves 15 to 20.

Paperwhite narcissus bulbs are easy to plant, and fast growing too!
Plant in pots four to six weeks before Christmas and you'll enjoy
their tiny white flowers on your holiday table.

Come In & Warm Up!

Lima Bean & Bacon Soup

Natalie Kopec
Mullica Hill, NJ

One of our favorite recipes to make on New Year's Eve! It's a family tradition that started after my husband & I were first married. We make it every year to celebrate the day.

16-oz. pkg. dried lima beans
3 to 4 carrots, peeled and sliced
4 redskin potatoes, sliced
1/2 c. onion, diced
1/2 c. red pepper, sliced
4 slices turkey bacon, sliced and
   crisply cooked

1-1/2 t. dried marjoram
1/2 t. dried oregano
1 t. salt
1/2 t. pepper
2 32-oz. containers low-sodium
   chicken broth, divided
1/4 c. butter, sliced

Cover beans with water; soak overnight. The next morning, drain beans. Place beans and remaining ingredients except broth and butter in a slow cooker. Add one container of broth and stir; add enough of remaining broth to cover beans. Add butter. Cover and cook on high setting for 3 to 4-1/2 hours, until beans are soft. Serves 10 to 12.

Twisty bread sticks are a tasty go-with for soup. Brush refrigerated bread stick dough with a little beaten egg and dust with Italian seasoning, then pop 'em in the oven and bake until toasty.

Mexican Minestrone

Ashley Billings
Shamong, NJ

A flavorful twist on traditional Italian minestrone.

3 14-oz. cans vegetable broth
2 15-1/2 oz. cans reduced-
    sodium black beans, drained
    and rinsed
15-oz. can garbanzo beans,
    drained and rinsed

2 to 3 tomatoes, chopped
2 c. potatoes, peeled and diced
2 c. frozen green beans
1 c. frozen corn
1 c. salsa
Garnish: sour cream

In a slow cooker, combine all ingredients except garnish; stir gently to mix. Cover and cook on low setting for 9 to 11 hours, or on high setting for 4-1/2 to 5-1/2 hours. Garnish individual bowls with sour cream. Makes 6 to 8 servings.

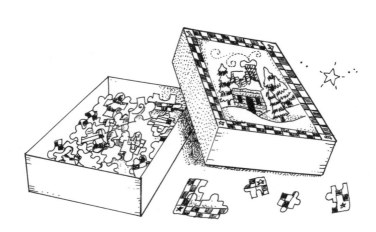

Start a new tradition! Lay out a Christmas-themed jigsaw puzzle early in December. Family members are sure to enjoy fitting a few pieces in place whenever they pass by.

Come In & Warm Up!

Cheesy White Chicken Chili

Holly Child
Parker, CO

I love to bring out this chili recipe when the weather starts getting chillier. It's so hearty and will warm you up on the coldest nights.

4 to 6 boneless, skinless chicken
    breasts, cooked and cubed
6 c. chicken broth
4 16-oz. cans Great Northern
    beans, drained and rinsed
4-oz. can green chiles

1 onion, chopped
1 T. garlic, minced
1 T. ground cumin
1-1/2 t. dried oregano
1-1/2 c. shredded Monterey
    Jack cheese

Combine all ingredients except cheese in a large slow cooker. Cover and cook on high setting for 4 to 6 hours. During the last hour, turn slow cooker to low setting. Stir in cheese; let stand for several minutes, until cheese is completely melted. Makes 8 servings.

Santa Fe Chicken Soup

Barb Griffith
Fort Collins, CO

Every Christmas Eve, when our family returns from church services we look forward to sitting down to our traditional soup supper.

16-oz. pkg. pasteurized process
    cheese spread, cubed
10-oz. can diced tomatoes with
    green chiles
1 lb. boneless, skinless chicken,
    cooked and cubed

15-1/2 oz. can pinto beans,
    drained and rinsed
14-1/2 oz. can stewed tomatoes
15-1/4 oz. can corn, drained
1 onion, chopped
corn chips or crackers

In a microwave-safe bowl, combine cheese and tomatoes with chiles. Cover and microwave on high setting for 5 minutes. Meanwhile, combine remaining ingredients in a large slow cooker. Stir cheese mixture; spoon into slow cooker. Cover and cook on high setting for 2 to 3 hours. Serve with corn chips or crackers. Serves 8 to 10.

Simple Vegetable Soup

Jane Hutfles
Omaha, NE

After the holidays, this light, tasty veggie-packed soup is a welcome meal! The longer it cooks, the more the flavor improves.

4 c. water
2 c. tomato juice
2 c. frozen green beans
1 c. cabbage, sliced
2 carrots, peeled and sliced
1 onion, sliced
1 stalk celery, sliced

2 cubes beef or vegetable
    bouillon
1 t. salt
pepper to taste
Optional: 1 T. soy sauce,
    1 t. sugar or sugar substitute

Combine all ingredients in a slow cooker. Cover and cook on low setting for 4 to 8 hours, until vegetables are tender. Serves 6.

Make a few notes on your brand-new calendar for next year's Christmas...places to go, people to see and things to do that you didn't get around to this year. When the holiday season rolls around again, you'll be glad you did!

A Cozy Christmas
Dinner

Rosemary Chicken Dinner

Vickie

A delicious one-pot family dinner with so little effort! Use either a whole roasting chicken or an equal amount of chicken pieces.

6 redskin potatoes, halved
3 carrots, peeled and thickly
   sliced
2 onions, cut into wedges

1/2 c. chicken broth
salt and pepper to taste
3-1/2 lbs. chicken
4 sprigs fresh rosemary

Combine vegetables in a large slow cooker; add broth. Sprinkle vegetables and chicken pieces with seasonings; add chicken to slow cooker. Place rosemary sprigs around chicken. Cover and cook on low setting for 7 to 9 hours, until chicken juices run clear when pierced. Makes 4 servings.

Make mini wreaths of rosemary to slip around dinner napkins.
Simply wind fresh rosemary stems into a ring shape, tuck in the ends
and tie on a tiny bow...so festive!

A Cozy Christmas Dinner

Mushroom Chicken

Kathy Rigg
Mount Sterling, IL

This is my go-to recipe. The mushrooms add such a rich flavor and it is a good looking dinner as well. Add a crisp salad or a steamed veggie and dinner is ready.

Optional: 1 T. oil
4 skinless, boneless chicken
  breasts
8-oz. pkg. white mushrooms,
  quartered
6-oz. pkg. shiitake mushrooms,
  stems removed and caps
  sliced
1/4 c. butter
0.7-oz. pkg. Italian salad
  dressing mix

10-3/4 oz. can golden
  mushroom soup
1/2 c. cream cheese
2 T. fresh chives, snipped
2 T. dried, minced onion
1/2 c. dry white wine or chicken
  broth
cooked angel hair pasta
Optional: chopped green onions

If desired, heat oil in a large skillet over medium heat; brown chicken on both sides. (Browning step may be omitted.) Combine mushrooms in a 4-quart slow cooker; top with chicken and set aside. Melt butter in a saucepan over medium heat; stir in dressing mix. Add soup, cream cheese, chives, onion and wine or broth; stir until cream cheese is melted. Spoon mixture over chicken. Cover and cook on low setting for 4 to 5 hours, until chicken juices run clear. Serve chicken and sauce over cooked pasta. If desired, sprinkle with green onions. Makes 4 servings.

Fill up the slow cooker with a hearty dinner in the morning. After supper, you'll be able to get an early start on a cozy family evening together, watching a favorite holiday movie like "A Christmas Story" or "Miracle on 34th Street."

Flavor-Bursting Pork Roast

Kelley Nicholson
Gooseberry Patch

*I've made this for my family over & over and everyone just loves it...
even my picky three-year-old! The onions become almost caramelized.
They are a sweet and delicious complement with each bite of the
tender pork.*

1 onion, sliced and separated
   into rings
2-1/2 lb. boneless pork
   loin roast
1 c. hot water
1/4 c. sugar
2 T. red wine vinegar

2 T. soy sauce
1 T. catsup
1/2 t. salt
1/2 t. pepper
1/4 t. garlic powder
1/8 t. hot pepper sauce,
   or to taste

Arrange onion slices evenly in the bottom of a slow cooker; place roast
on top. In a bowl, mix together remaining ingredients; stir until sugar
dissolves and pour over roast. Cover and cook on low setting for 6 to
8 hours, or on high setting for 3 to 4 hours, until pork is tender.
Serves 4 to 6.

Cranberry Sweet Potatoes

Jody Keiper
Crystal Lake, IL

*This easy dish makes its own delicious cranberry sauce
while it cooks. It's sweet, tangy and healthy...wonderful with
roast chicken, turkey or pork.*

3 to 4 sweet potatoes, peeled
   and cubed
12-oz. pkg. fresh cranberries
1 c. pure maple syrup

3 T. butter, cubed
1 t. cinnamon
1/2 t. salt

Combine all ingredients in a slow cooker; stir gently. Cover and cook
on low setting for 6 hours, or on high setting for 3 hours. Serves 8.

A Cozy Christmas Dinner

Cranberry-Cola Pork Chops

Rachel Dingler
Swartz Creek, MI

This is my very own recipe. Slow cooking the pork chops with cola makes them so tender! I like to serve them with cranberry stuffing and thick slices of French bread on the side.

4 thick-cut pork chops
salt and pepper to taste
2 c. cola (not diet)

2 14-oz. cans jellied cranberry
   sauce

Trim any fat from chops; rub with salt and pepper. Set aside. In a bowl, gently whisk together cola and cranberry sauce until well blended. Add one cup of cranberry mixture to a slow cooker, spreading to cover the bottom evenly. Place chops in slow cooker; top with remaining cranberry mixture. Cover and cook on low setting for 6 to 8 hours, or on high setting for 3 to 4 hours. Serve pork chops topped with glaze from slow cooker, if desired. Makes 4 servings.

Cheesy Spinach Casserole

Marian Forck
Chamois, MO

This dish is so good, even spinach haters will love it!

2 10-oz. pkgs. frozen chopped
   spinach, thawed and drained
2 c. cottage cheese
3 eggs, beaten

1-1/2 c. shredded Cheddar
   cheese
1/2 c. butter, softened
1/4 c. all-purpose flour

Mix all ingredients in a greased slow cooker. Cover and cook on high setting for one hour; reduce to low setting and cook for 4 to 6 hours. Makes 6 to 8 servings.

Bring a bit of retro to the holiday kitchen...tie on a vintage Christmas apron!

Mom's Pot Roast

Cynthia Stuckey
Wake Forest, NC

As a newlywed with a husband in graduate school, this became one of our favorites. I always loved to serve this as I could spend a few minutes in the morning putting it in the slow cooker, and come home in time for dinner to the lovely aroma of pot roast and vegetables. The roast makes its own gravy, so after whipping up mashed potatoes, your dinner is complete! It feeds a crowd and makes excellent leftovers.

3 to 4-lb. boneless beef chuck
    roast
garlic salt and pepper to taste
1/2 lb. whole or sliced
    mushrooms
1 onion, cut into thin wedges

1.35-oz. pkg. onion soup mix
1/2 lb. baby carrots
10-3/4 oz. can cream of
    mushroom soup
Optional: 1 to 2 T. all-purpose
    flour

Rub roast on both sides with garlic salt and pepper; place in a large slow cooker. Top roast with mushrooms and onion; sprinkle with soup mix. Add carrots; spoon soup over carrots. Cover and cook on low setting for 8 to 10 hours, until roast is tender. Remove roast and vegetables to a serving platter; serve with cooking liquid for gravy. If a thicker gravy is desired, whisk flour into cooking liquid until gravy reaches desired consistency. Cover and cook on high setting, until thickened. Makes 8 servings.

Food for friends doesn't have to be fancy. Your guests will be delighted with comfort foods like Grandma used to make. Invite them to help themselves from large platters set right on the table...so family-friendly and a perfect time to use your holiday dishes.

A Cozy Christmas Dinner

Simple Beef Stroganoff

Therese Stewart
Toronto, Ontario

This is such an easy meal to make, and it's one of our family favorites. There are happy faces and full tummies each time I prepare it!

1 lb. beef sirloin, cut into
   bite-size cubes
1.35-oz. pkg. onion soup mix
10-3/4 oz. can cream of
   mushroom soup

2 8-oz. pkgs. sliced mushrooms
1 clove garlic, minced
8-oz. container sour cream
cooked wide egg noodles

Combine all ingredients except sour cream and noodles in a slow cooker. Cover and cook on low setting for 8 to 10 hours, until beef is tender. Shortly before serving time, stir in sour cream; heat through. To serve, ladle stroganoff over cooked noodles. Makes 6 servings.

When buying a fresh tree, be sure to take home any boughs cut from the base of the tree. Nothing says Christmas like fresh touches of greenery sprinkled throughout your home!

Busy-Day Spinach Lasagna

Teresa Eller
Tonganoxie, KS

Great for having ready in advance, working late and company coming. Dinner will be ready when you get home from work... just add some garlic toast and a crisp salad.

2 lbs. extra-lean ground beef
2 T. Italian seasoning, divided
2 14-1/2 oz. cans diced tomatoes, divided
2 8-oz. cans tomato sauce, divided

6 c. fresh spinach, torn and divided
3 c. shredded Swiss or mozzarella cheese, divided
12-oz. pkg. lasagna noodles, uncooked and broken up

Break up uncooked beef and place in a slow cooker sprayed with non-stick vegetable spray. Sprinkle beef with one tablespoon Italian seasoning. Add one can tomatoes with juice and one can tomato sauce; stir gently to combine. Add half of spinach; press down gently. Add one cup cheese and half of uncooked noodles. Repeat layers, ending with cheese on top. Cover and cook on low setting for 8 hours. Makes 6 to 8 servings.

Set a teeny-tiny snowman at each person's place...so cute! Simply glue white pompoms together with craft glue, then add faces and scarves clipped from bits of felt.

A Cozy Christmas Dinner

Italian-Style Vegetables

Tori Willis
Champaign, IL

A scrumptious side dish, or for a meatless main, ladle the vegetable mixture over cooked pasta or squares of polenta.

1 eggplant, peeled and cut in
  1-inch cubes
2 to 3 zucchini, halved
  lengthwise and sliced
  1/2-inch thick
1 t. salt
1 T. olive oil
3/4 lb. sliced mushrooms

1 onion, sliced thinly
4 roma tomatoes, sliced
1-1/2 c. shredded Italian-blend
  cheese
2 c. tomato sauce
1 t. dried oregano
salt and pepper to taste

In a bowl, toss eggplant and zucchini with salt. Place in a large colander; set over bowl to drain for one hour. Squeeze out excess moisture. Heat oil in a large skillet over medium heat. Add eggplant, zucchini, mushrooms and onion; sauté just until tender. In a slow cooker, layer 1/3 each of vegetable mixture, tomatoes, tomato sauce, seasonings and cheese. Repeat layers 2 more times, ending with cheese on top. Cover and cook on low setting for 6 to 8 hours, until vegetables are tender. Serves 6 to 8.

Even if your fireplace isn't being used during the holidays, it can still look warm and inviting. Fill an empty grate with cheerful wrapped packages, candles of every shape and size or snowy-white birch logs accented by shiny ornaments.

Mrs. Ross's Hearty Ribs

Kelly Ross
Coventry, CT

My husband Michael is not a big fan of our cold New England winters. So, one snowy, bitterly cold day, I cooked up this easy, yet delicious meal. He loved it so much, he asked if I could make it every time there's a blizzard. I agreed, and now he looks forward to the snow!

3-1/2 to 4 lbs. country-style
   pork ribs
16-oz. bottle Catalina salad
   dressing
1-1/2 T. dark brown sugar,
   packed

40-oz. bottle favorite barbecue
   sauce, divided
2 sweet onions, sliced
Optional: cooked rice

Place ribs in a large slow cooker sprayed with non-stick vegetable spray. In a large bowl, mix salad dressing, brown sugar and 3/4 of barbecue sauce. Spoon mixture over ribs. Place onions on top. With a large spoon, press onions gently into sauce mixture. Cover and cook on low setting for 8 to 9 hours, until ribs are tender. Serve with cooked rice, if desired. Serves 4.

Cheesy Hashbrown Casserole

Becky Butler
Keller, TX

Delicious, incredibly easy and doesn't take up valuable oven space during holiday meal preparations! What more could you want?

32-oz. pkg. frozen diced
   potatoes, thawed
2 10-3/4 oz. cans Cheddar
   cheese soup

12-oz. can evaporated milk
3-oz. can French fried onion
   rings, divided
salt and pepper to taste

Spray a slow cooker with non-stick vegetable spray. Add potatoes, soup, milk and onion rings, reserving 1/4 cup onion rings for topping. Season with salt and pepper; stir gently. Cover and cook on low setting for 6 to 7 hours, or on high setting for 3 to 4 hours. Sprinkle reserved onions over top just before serving. Serves 8.

A Cozy Christmas Dinner

Slow-Cooked Cola Ribs

Stephanie Carlson
Sioux Falls, SD

I first tried this recipe a couple of years ago, mostly out of curiosity. It's become my tried & true recipe for pork ribs and my family loves it. It not only produces tender, delicious pork ribs, it's super easy, and uses just a few ingredients!

2 lbs. country-style pork ribs
salt and pepper to taste
12-oz. can cola (not diet)

18-oz. bottle favorite barbecue
   sauce

Generously season ribs with salt and pepper. Place ribs in a large slow cooker sprayed with non-stick vegetable spray; pour cola over top. Cover and cook on low setting for 6 to 8 hours, until ribs are tender. With a slotted spoon, remove ribs to a platter. Drain cooking liquid from slow cooker; return ribs to the crock. Cover ribs with desired amount of barbecue sauce; cover and cook another 15 to 20 minutes, until warmed through. Serves 4.

If your slow cooker doesn't have a built-in timer, pick up an automatic timer at the hardware store and plug the crock right into it. It's also fine to fill a slow cooker with chilled ingredients, then set the crock's timer to start one to 2 hours later.

Mrs. Spears's Beef & Noodles

Tamela James
Grove City, OH

Mrs. Spears was a wonderful lady in our church who made this dish for my mom when Mom was sick. It has become a family favorite because it is so easy and gets rave reviews. It's terrific for Sunday after church, a busy weeknight or to take along to a potluck. Need to serve a few more people? Just add another can of soup and a few more noodles.

4 to 5-lb. boneless beef
   chuck roast
1 lb. sliced mushrooms
3 carrots, peeled and sliced
1 onion, quartered
2 10-3/4 oz. cans cream of
   mushroom soup

10-3/4 oz. can cream of celery
   soup
1-1/4 c. milk or water
3 cloves garlic, minced
16-oz. pkg. egg noodles, cooked

Place roast in a lightly greased large slow cooker; surround with vegetables and set aside. In a large bowl, stir together remaining ingredients except noodles; spoon over roast. Cover and cook on high setting for 6 to 8 hours, until roast is tender. Stir to break up roast into pieces. Add cooked noodles to slow cooker; stir gently to coat with gravy. Makes 8 to 10 servings.

Place a guest book on the table alongside a jar filled with colored pens. Encourage everyone to sign it...even small kids can draw a picture. Add favorite photos and you'll have a holiday scrapbook in no time!

A Cozy Christmas Dinner

Hungarian Goulash

Jeanne Caia
Ontario, NY

This delicious recipe was passed down to me from my mom.
If your family doesn't care for diced tomatoes, you can use
a can of tomato sauce instead.

2 lbs. beef round steak, cut into
   1/2-inch cubes
1 c. onion, chopped
1 clove garlic, minced
2 T. all-purpose flour
14-1/2 oz. can diced tomatoes
1/2 t. salt

1/2 t. pepper
1-1/2 t. paprika
1/4 t. dried thyme
1 bay leaf
8-oz. container sour cream
cooked egg noodles

Add beef, onion and garlic to a slow cooker. Sprinkle with flour; mix
well to coat. Add undrained tomatoes and seasonings; stir gently to
mix. Tuck in bay leaf. Cover and cook on low setting for 8 to 10 hours,
or on high setting for 4 to 5 hours. About 30 minutes before serving
time, discard bay leaf; stir in sour cream. Serve goulash over cooked
noodles. Makes 8 servings.

If the kids just can't wait 'til Christmas, celebrate early on St. Nicholas Day,
December 6th! Each child sets out their shoes the night before...St. Nick will
fill the shoes of those who've behaved with treats and small presents. Or make
the holiday last just a little longer by putting out shoes on January 6th,
when the Three Kings come to fill them.

Seasoned Turkey Breast

Kay Helbert
Castlewood, VA

This is so simple and one of my favorites. The turkey is very tender and flavorful...it makes fabulous sandwiches, if there's any left!

1 t. dried thyme	1 t. salt
1 t. dried rosemary	1 t. pepper
1 t. onion powder	7-lb. bone-in turkey breast,
1 t. garlic powder	thawed if frozen

Combine all seasonings in a cup; sprinkle over turkey. Place turkey in slow cooker; do not add any liquid. Cover and cook on low setting for 10 to 12 hours, or overnight, until turkey is tender and juices run clear when pierced. Remove turkey to a serving platter; let stand for several minutes before slicing. Serves 8.

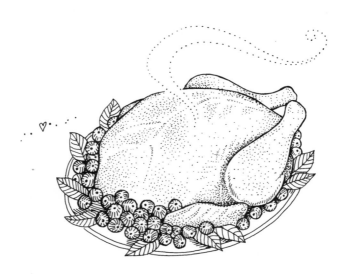

A sparkling garnish for your holiday turkey...sugared cranberries.
Brush whole berries with light corn syrup, then roll in coarse sugar.

A Cozy Christmas Dinner

Cornbread Dressing

Becky Butler
Keller, TX

This is a terrific side dish to make in the slow cooker. It frees up oven space for other holiday essentials, and stays warm in the crock after it's finished cooking.

8 slices white bread, cubed
10 to 12-inch pan baked
   cornbread
2 10-3/4 oz. cans cream of
   chicken soup
4 eggs, beaten

1 onion, finely chopped
1/2 c. celery, finely chopped
2 t. poultry seasoning
1/2 to 1 t. pepper
2 T. butter, sliced

Place bread cubes on a baking sheet; let stand overnight, until stale. Crumble cornbread into a large bowl. Add bread cubes and remaining ingredients except butter. Mix well; spoon into a large greased slow cooker and spread evenly. Dot with butter. Cover and cook on low setting for 4 hours, or on high setting for 2 hours, until heated through Serves 10 to 12.

Grandma's Cranberry Sauce

Michelle Powell
Valley, AL

Grandma always jarred this fresh cranberry sauce around Thanksgiving. Now I make it every year to enjoy all winter long. A jar of cranberry sauce makes a great Christmas gift too!

2 oranges, chopped
2 oranges, peeled and chopped
4 apples, cored and chopped

2 lbs. fresh cranberries
1 c. sugar

Combine all ingredients in a large slow cooker; stir gently. Cover and cook on low setting for 8 to 9 hours, stirring occasionally, until syrupy and berries have burst. Spoon into freezer containers or sterilized jars. Cover and refrigerate for up to 3 weeks, or freeze for up to 3 months. Makes about 8 pints.

Honey-Dijon Ham

Gladys Kielar
Whitehouse, OH

*A delicious ham that can't be beat. Serve it for your holiday dinner,
then enjoy the leftovers as sandwiches...that's really the best part!*

5-lb. fully cooked bone-in ham
1/3 c. apple juice
1/4 c. brown sugar, packed

1 T. honey
1 T. Dijon mustard

Place ham in a large slow cooker. Mix apple juice, brown sugar, honey
and mustard in a small bowl; spread over ham. Cover and cook on low
setting for 8 hours, or until heated through. Remove ham to a serving
platter. Slice and serve with sauce from slow cooker. Makes 10 to
12 servings.

Kyra's Glazed Ham

Shannon Reents
Loudonville, OH

*My daughter-in-law gave me this recipe one Christmas Eve.
It's a keeper...I love it!*

10 to 14-lb. fully cooked
   bone-in ham
2/3 c. honey

1-1/4 c. brown sugar, packed
1 c. hot water

Pierce ham all over with a fork; spread honey over ham and place in a
very large slow cooker. In a bowl, mix brown sugar and hot water;
pour over ham. Cover and cook on low setting for about 8 hours.
Serves 20 to 24.

If you're having trouble fitting your ham into the slow cooker, trim a bit off
the side with your knife and lay the ham on its side. Save any ham trimmings
to add to tomorrow's scrambled eggs. It's a perfect solution!

A Cozy Christmas Dinner

Old-Fashioned Scalloped Corn

Laurel Perry
Loganville, GA

*This is a popular recipe I make at the holidays. It's so easy
to take to family get-togethers and everyone enjoys it.*

2/3 c. all-purpose flour
5-oz. can evaporated milk
1 c. egg substitute or eggs,
　beaten
1/3 c. butter, melted and
　slightly cooled

14-3/4 oz. can cream-style corn
2 c. frozen corn, thawed and
　drained
1 T. sugar
1/2 t. salt
1/8 t. pepper

In a bowl, whisk together flour and evaporated milk until smooth.
Whisk in eggs, then melted butter. Stir in remaining ingredients. Pour
into a slow cooker coated with non-stick vegetable spray. Cover and
cook on high setting for 2 to 3 hours, until firm. Serves 8.

When setting a children's table for Christmas dinner, make it playful!
Cover the tabletop with giftwrap, decorate paper cups and napkins
with holiday stickers and add a gingerbread house centerpiece...
the kids will beg to sit there!

Jennifer's Chicken Stuff

Jennifer Sievers
Carol Stream, IL

The first time I made this hearty dish for dinner, it was a hit with both my daughters. A week later, the younger one asked me to make "that chicken stuff" again and the name just stuck!

1 onion, diced
2 carrots, peeled and diced
2 stalks celery, diced
6 boneless, skinless chicken
    breasts

2 c. brown rice, uncooked
32-oz. container chicken broth
salt and pepper to taste

In a slow cooker, layer all ingredients except salt and pepper in order listed. Cover and cook on low setting for about 8 hours, until chicken is very tender. Stir well to break up chicken and mix everything together. Season with salt and pepper to taste. Serves 6.

Wrapping up a slow cooker as a gift for a new bride? Jot down all your favorite, tried & true slow-cooker recipes and tuck 'em inside. A thoughtful gift that's sure to be appreciated!

A Cozy Christmas Dinner

No-Fuss Chicken Dinner

Erin Hibshman
Lebanon, PA

Perfect for those busy days when everyone has someplace else to be...it tastes as if you spent hours over the stove!

4 to 6 chicken breasts
4 baking potatoes, quartered
1/2 lb. baby carrots
1 onion, chopped

10-3/4 oz. can cream of chicken
  soup
1/4 t. garlic powder
2 to 4 T. water

Place chicken in a large slow cooker; arrange vegetables around chicken. In a bowl, stir together soup, garlic powder and enough water to make it pourable. Spoon soup mixture over chicken and vegetables. Cover and cook on low setting for 7 to 8 hours, stirring once after 4 hours, if possible. Makes 4 to 6 servings.

Stir up some memories...invite Grandma & Grandpa to read Christmas stories to little ones and share holiday stories from their childhood.

Cheesy Chicken Ranch Nachos

Melissa Flasck
Sterling Heights, MI

Great for working moms. It's quick & easy to toss together in the morning, and gives me more time to play with my son!

1-1/2 lbs. boneless, skinless
   chicken breasts or thighs
2 10-3/4 oz. cans Cheddar
   cheese soup
1-1/2 c. chicken broth
1 c. salsa

15-1/4 oz. can corn
tortilla chips
Garnish: ranch salad dressing
Optional: extra salsa or hot
   pepper sauce

Place chicken in a slow cooker; top with soup and salsa. Cover and cook on low setting for 8 hours, on high setting for 4 hours. Add corn in the last 30 minutes of cooking. Shred chicken with 2 forks and return to slow cooker. To serve, cover dinner plates with tortilla chips; ladle chicken mixture over chips and drizzle with salad dressing. Top with salsa or hot sauce, if desired. Serves 4.

Mexican Hominy

Mary Stephenson
Grovespring, MO

A side dish for your favorite Mexican dinner that's just a bit different! Make it milder or hotter simply by using different chiles.

2 15-1/2 oz. cans yellow
   hominy, drained
2 15-1/2 oz. cans white
   hominy, drained
4-oz. can chopped green chiles

8-oz. container sour cream
1 c. shredded Colby cheese
1/2 t. onion powder
1/4 t. garlic powder
salt to taste

Combine all ingredients in a greased slow cooker. Cover and cook on low setting for 2 to 3 hours, until hot and bubbly. Serves 8.

Make dinner easy with do-it-yourself tacos. Set out taco shells, seasoned beef and muffin tins filled with all the fixin's. Quick, tasty and fun!

A Cozy Christmas Dinner

Easy Carnitas

Christine Arrieta
Aurora, CO

When I was a teenager, burritos were my food of choice. My school didn't sell candy at fundraisers, we sold homemade burritos and tortas. My kids like to do the same, but with busy schedules it's not always easy. With this recipe, you can get that traditional flavor without much effort! This flavorful pork can be used to prepare various Mexican dishes.

4 to 5-lb. boneless pork
    shoulder butt roast
seasoned meat tenderizer, salt
    and pepper to taste
2 T. olive oil

1/2 onion, chopped
2 cloves garlic, minced
28-oz. can green enchilada
    sauce

Sprinkle roast generously with tenderizer, salt and pepper; set aside. Heat oil in a large skillet over medium heat. Sauté onion for 2 minutes, or just until translucent. Add garlic; cook for one additional minute. Push onion and garlic to edge of skillet; add roast and brown on all sides. Transfer roast to a large slow cooker; top with onion mixture and enchilada sauce. Cover and cook on low setting for 8 hours, or on high setting for 3 hours, until pork is fork-tender. Shred roast with 2 forks; serve as desired in tacos, burritos and on nachos. Makes 10 to 12 servings.

Variation:

For a traditional finish to your carnitas, spoon shredded pork onto an aluminum foil-lined baking sheet. Top with several spoonfuls of sauce. Broil for 5 to 10 minutes, until edges of pork are golden.

Send Christmas postcards instead of ordinary cards...they're fun to send, quick to write and cost less to mail. Pick up some sweet old-timey reproductions or make your own...either way, they're sure to be enjoyed!

Italian Mozzarella Chicken

Cindy Jamieson
Barrie, Ontario

Being a busy mom, my slow cooker comes in handy. I've turned a family favorite into a healthy slow-cooked meal.

4 boneless, skinless chicken
   breasts
salt and pepper
1/2 t. dried oregano
1/2 t. dried basil
3 cloves garlic, minced

2 c. marinara sauce
1 c. shredded mozzarella cheese
8-oz. pkg. penne pasta, cooked
1/3 c. green olives with
   pimentos, chopped
1/4 c. grated Parmesan cheese

Season chicken breasts on both sides with salt, pepper and herbs. Place chicken in a slow cooker; sprinkle with garlic and top with marinara sauce. Cover and cook on low setting for 6 hours, or until chicken is tender. Remove chicken to a lightly greased baking sheet; top with mozzarella cheese and set aside. About 30 minutes before serving, cook pasta according to package directions; drain. Add olives and Parmesan cheese to sauce in slow cooker, cover and heat through. Broil chicken until cheese is melted and toasted. Toss cooked pasta with sauce; serve with chicken. Serves 4.

Jump-start tomorrow's dinner! Chop and assemble ingredients tonight... refrigerate meat and veggies in separate containers.

A Cozy Christmas Dinner

Bowtie Lasagna Casserole

Kristi Magowan
Greenwich, NY

I love making this dish for holiday potluck dinners...it seems we're always invited to contribute to several every year! It can feed a crowd and it's a perfect main or side dish. Serve with crusty bread and a light salad for a satisfying meal.

1 lb. ground beef
1 T. olive oil
1 onion, chopped
2 t. garlic, chopped
28-oz. can crushed tomatoes
8-oz. can tomato sauce
1 T. brown sugar, packed
1 T. dried oregano
salt and pepper to taste
8-oz. pkg. bowtie pasta, uncooked
15-oz. container ricotta cheese
1 c. shredded mozzarella cheese
Garnish: grated Parmesan cheese

In a skillet over medium heat, cook beef until no longer pink. Drain; add to a slow cooker. Add olive oil and onion to skillet; cook until translucent, 5 to 7 minutes. Add garlic; cook for one minute. Spoon onion mixture over beef; stir in undrained tomatoes, tomato sauce, brown sugar and seasonings. Cover and cook on low setting for 6 to 7 hours. About 30 minutes before serving, cook pasta according to package directions; drain. Add cooked pasta and ricotta cheese to sauce in slow cooker; stir to combine. Top with mozzarella cheese. Turn slow cooker to high setting. Cover and cook for an additional 30 minutes, until heated through and cheese is melted. Serve garnished with Parmesan cheese. Makes 8 to 12 servings.

After Christmas dinner, a simple dessert is perfect. Enjoy a platter of assorted Christmas cookies accompanied by scoops of pink peppermint ice cream.

Best-Ever Chicken & Noodles

Kathy Evans
Quinter, KS

My daughter and I like to try new recipes together. We think these are the best and easiest chicken & noodles we've ever tasted!

3 boneless, skinless chicken breasts
2 10-3/4 oz. cans cream of chicken soup
3 14-oz. cans chicken broth

1/2 c. margarine, sliced
12-oz. pkg. wide egg noodles, uncooked
Optional: mashed potatoes

Combine chicken, soup, broth and margarine in a large slow cooker. Cover and cook on low setting for 8 hours, or on high setting for 4 hours, until chicken is very tender. Shred chicken; stir into mixture in slow cooker along with uncooked noodles. Cover and cook until noodles are tender, about 45 minutes. Serve on dinner plates, ladled over mashed potatoes, or ladle into soup bowls. Makes about 8 servings.

Honey-Glazed Chicken

Joshua Logan
Victoria, TX

A terrific make-ahead when tomorrow is a busy day!

8 pieces chicken
1/2 c. honey

1/4 c. butter, melted
2 T. soy sauce

Place chicken in a large plastic zipping bag. Drizzle with remaining ingredients; seal bag and squeeze to coat. Freeze. To prepare, thaw overnight in refrigerator. Add contents to a slow cooker. Cover and cook on low setting for about 8 hours, until chicken juices run clear. Makes 8 servings.

Tuck silverware into plush red mini Christmas stockings to lay on each guest's plate...how festive!

A Cozy Christmas Dinner

Company Mashed Potatoes

Gloria Kaufmann
Orrville, OH

Mashed potatoes are the best comfort food ever. I love that these wonderful tasting potatoes can be made two to three hours before company arrives...no last-minute preparation!

5 lbs. redskin potatoes,
   quartered
1 T. garlic, minced, or to taste
3 cubes chicken bouillon
1 to 2 t. salt

8-oz. container sour cream
8-oz. pkg. cream cheese,
   softened
1/3 c. butter, sliced
salt and pepper to taste

In a saucepan over medium-high heat, cover potatoes with water; add garlic, bouillon and salt. Bring to a boil; cook until potatoes are tender, about 15 to 20 minutes. Drain, reserving cooking water. Mash potatoes with sour cream and cream cheese to desired consistency, adding reserved water as needed. Transfer potato mixture to a slow cooker. Cover and cook on low setting for 2 to 3 hours. Just before serving, stir in butter; season with salt and pepper. Makes 10 to 12 servings.

The more the merrier! Why not invite a neighbor or a college student who might be spending the holiday alone to share in the Christmas feast?

Creamy Chicken & Rice

Wanda Boykin
Lewisburg, TN

So easy to make...delicious on a cold winter day!

3 to 4 boneless, skinless chicken
   breasts, cubed
10-3/4 oz. can cream of chicken
   soup
14-oz. can chicken broth

1/2 c. onion, chopped
3 c. long-cooking rice, uncooked
3 c. water
salt and pepper to taste

Combine all ingredients in a slow cooker; stir gently to mix. Cover and cook on low setting for 4 to 6 hours, until chicken is no longer pink and rice is tender. Makes 6 to 8 servings.

Need a quick hostess gift? Tuck a little herb plant into a dainty
thrift-shop teacup. Wrap it up in cellophane and add a jolly note...
easy, sweet and long lasting.

A Cozy Christmas Dinner

Pork Chops & Tomato Rice

Janice Hardin
Lincoln, NE

*My mother used to fix this recipe and it was the first recipe
I ever made for my husband when we were dating.
It always turns out perfect!*

4 pork chops
1 T. oil
1 to 2 t. oil
salt and pepper to taste
10-3/4 oz. can tomato soup
3/4 c. long-cooking rice,

uncooked
1 c. boiling water
1/3 c. onion, finely chopped
1/3 c. green pepper, chopped
1/4 t. Worcestershire sauce
1/2 t. salt

In a skillet over medium heat, brown pork chops in hot oil. Season
with salt and pepper; place in a slow cooker. Combine remaining
ingredients in a bowl; spoon evenly over pork chops. Cover and cook
on low setting for 6 to 8 hours. Add a little more water if mixture gets
too dry. Makes 4 servings.

Slow-cooker meals are perfect after a day of Christmas shopping. For an easy
side, whip up a marinated salad to keep in the fridge...cut up crunchy
veggies and toss with zesty Italian salad dressing.

Honeyed Cranberry Pork Roast

Rogene Rogers
Bemidji, MN

I love cranberries for the holidays! First thing on Christmas Eve morning, I put this roast in the slow cooker and give myself more time to spend with my family. Serve with cinnamon-sprinkled sweet potatoes.

3 to 4-lb. pork roast
salt and pepper to taste
1-1/2 c. fresh cranberries, finely
   chopped

1/2 c. honey
2 t. orange zest
1/4 t. ground cloves
1/2 t. nutmeg

Season roast on all sides with salt and pepper; place in a slow cooker. Combine remaining ingredients in a bowl; spoon over roast. Cover and cook on low setting for 8 to 10 hours, until roast is tender and no longer pink inside. Makes 8 servings.

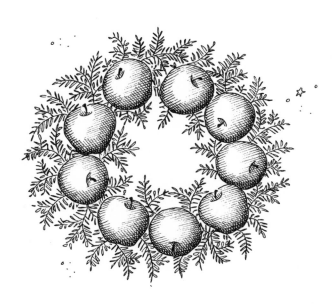

Deck the front door with a little unexpected color...secure bright green Granny Smith apples with wire to a traditional greenery wreath.

A Cozy Christmas Dinner

Apple-Spiced Sweet Potatoes

Amanda Charlton
Port Alberni, British Columbia

*Candied pecans make an extra special topping
for this holiday side dish.*

3-1/2 to 4 lbs. sweet potatoes,
   cut into 2-inch cubes
21-oz. can apple pie filling
1/3 c. golden raisins

5 T. butter, diced and divided
1-1/2 t. apple pie spice
1 c. chopped pecans
1/3 c. sugar

Lightly coat a 4-quart slow cooker with cooking spray. Add sweet potatoes, pie filling, raisins, 3 tablespoons butter and spice; mix well. Cover and cook on low setting for 6 to 8 hours, or on high setting for 3 to 4 hours. Meanwhile, combine remaining butter, pecans and sugar in a skillet. Cook over medium heat, stirring constantly, for 8 to 10 minutes, until sugar turns golden, starts to melt and sticks to pecans. Pour candied pecan mixture onto aluminum foil and let cool completely; crush coarsely. Top potatoes with pecan mixture before serving. Makes 8 to 10 servings.

Remember the true meaning of Christmas. Set out a creche with sturdy nativity figures for your kids to add, one per day, leading up to Baby Jesus on Christmas Day.

Turkey & Ham Cordon Bleu

Rebecca Etling
Blairsville, PA

This is a wonderful recipe using leftovers! I love to make it the day after Christmas before I go shopping the after-holiday sales. I also make it year 'round...it's a real family favorite.

10-3/4 oz. can cream of chicken
   soup
2 T. stone-ground mustard with
   horseradish
2 c. cooked turkey, cubed

1 c. cooked ham, cubed
2 6-oz. pkgs. turkey-flavored
   stuffing mix, prepared, or
   6 to 7 c. leftover stuffing
8 slices Swiss cheese

Blend soup and mustard in a bowl; spread in the bottom of a slow cooker. Add turkey and ham. Spoon stuffing over top; layer with cheese slices. Cover and cook on low setting for 4 hours, or until mixture is heated through and cheese is melted. Serves 6 to 8.

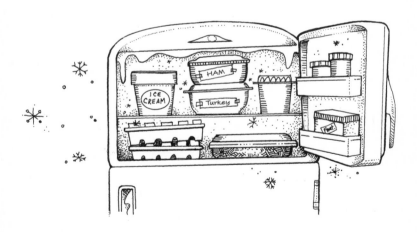

Do you have lots of leftover holiday turkey or ham? It freezes well for up to three months. Cut into bite-size pieces, place in plastic freezer bags and pop in the freezer...ready to stir into hearty casseroles or soups whenever you are!

A Cozy Christmas Dinner

Mushroom Wild Rice

*Stephanie Mayer
Portsmouth, VA*

A savory side dish to set & forget.

10-1/2 oz. can beef consommé
10-1/2 oz. can French onion
   soup
3 4-oz. cans sliced mushrooms,
   drained

1 c. long-cooking brown rice,
   uncooked
1 c. wild rice, uncooked
2-1/4 c. water
1/2 c. butter, melted

Combine all ingredients in a slow cooker; stir well. Cover and cook on low setting for 7 to 8 hours, until rice is tender. Serves 8 to 10.

Bacon-Cheese Potatoes

*Coleen Lambert
Luxemburg, WI*

A super-easy version of everybody's favorite potatoes.

1/4 lb. bacon, diced
2 onions, thinly sliced
4 potatoes, peeled and thinly
   sliced
salt and pepper to taste

4 to 6 T. butter, sliced
8-oz. pkg. shredded Cheddar
   cheese
Garnish: sliced green onions

Line a slow cooker with aluminum foil, leaving enough to fold over the top. Layer half each of bacon, onions and potatoes; season with salt and pepper and dot with butter. Repeat layers; fold aluminum foil over top. Cover and cook on low setting for 4 to 6 hours; check for doneness after 4 hours. About 20 to 30 minutes before serving, uncover and fold back foil; top with cheese. Cover and cook until cheese is melted; sprinkle with green onions. Makes 4 servings.

Share the bubbly! Kids will feel extra-special when served sparkling white grape juice or ginger ale in long-stemmed plastic glasses.

Fruited Roast Pork

Melody Taynor
Everett, WA

I was looking for something just a little different to serve for Christmas dinner...I'm glad I found this easy and delicious recipe!

1 onion, sliced
2-lb. boneless pork loin roast
7-oz. pkg. mixed dried fruit,
   coarsely chopped

3/4 c. apple cider
1/2 t. nutmeg
1/4 t. cinnamon
1/2 t. salt

Place onion slices in the bottom of a slow cooker. Add roast; top with fruit. Mix remaining ingredients in a cup; drizzle over roast. Cover and cook on low setting for 6 to 8 hours, until pork is tender. Remove roast to a serving platter; let stand several minutes before slicing. Serve sliced roast topped with fruit sauce from slow cooker. Serves 6 to 8.

Enjoy a winter weekend retreat at home! Tuck dinner in the slow cooker, then spend the day in your jammies...savor a leisurely brunch, do puzzles, browse holiday catalogs or re-read a favorite book. What could be cozier?

A Cozy Christmas Dinner

Mom's Best-Ever Baked Beans

Gloria Smith
Webster, MA

My mom made this recipe every week for over 40 years. The family would gather on Saturdays to eat hot dogs and her beans. Mom is in her 80's now and our families have all moved in different directions, but all of us girls still carry on the tradition and make Mom's beans for our family & friends.

16-oz. pkg. dried pea or
   navy beans
1 onion, chopped
1/3 c. brown sugar, packed

2 T. catsup
2 T. molasses, or more to taste
1/2 t. dry mustard
1 t. salt

Cover beans with water; soak overnight. In the morning, drain; add beans and remaining ingredients to a slow cooker. Stir; add enough water to cover beans. Cover and cook on low setting for 8 hours, or until beans are tender. Serves 8 to 10.

Aunt Judy's Red-Hot Applesauce

Sandy Coffey
Cincinnati, OH

A delicious, fun recipe for Thanksgiving and Christmas from way back when! It's extra easy and the whole clan loves it.

5 lbs. red apples, peeled, cored
   and sliced
1/4 c. butter, sliced

16-oz. pkg. red cinnamon
   candies, divided

Place apples in a large slow cooker. Cover and cook on high setting for about 3 hours, until soft and tender. Stir in butter and half of candies; let stand until candies melt and apples turn red. Add more candies to taste. Mash apples to desired consistency with a potato masher or fork. Serve warm. Makes 8 to 10 servings.

Slow-Cooked Meatloaf

Tina Goodpasture
Meadowview, VA

Try this recipe just once...you'll never make meatloaf another way!

2 eggs, beaten
3/4 c. milk
3 slices bread, torn into small
   pieces
1 t. salt
1/2 t. pepper

1 c. catsup, divided
2 lbs. ground beef
1/2 c. onion, diced
1-oz. pkg. ranch salad
   dressing mix

In a large bowl, mix eggs, milk, bread crumbs, salt and pepper; let stand for 20 minutes. Add 1/2 cup catsup and remaining ingredients. Mix gently; mound in a greased slow cooker. Spread remaining catsup over top. Cover and cook on high setting for 15 minutes. Turn to low setting and cook for 7 hours. Serves 6 to 8.

All-Day Mac & Cheese

Laurie Ruell
Rochester, NY

So much better than a mix...rich, creamy and the kids love it!

8-oz. pkg. elbow macaroni,
   uncooked
16-oz. pkg. shredded sharp
   Cheddar cheese, divided
12-oz. can evaporated milk

1-1/2 c. milk
2 eggs, beaten
1 t. salt
1/2 t. pepper

Cook macaroni according to package directions, just until tender; drain and transfer to a large bowl. Add 3 cups cheese and remaining ingredients. Mix well; spoon into a slow cooker coated with non-stick vegetable spray. Sprinkle with remaining cheese. Cover and cook on low setting for 5 to 6 hours, until firm and edges are golden. Makes 4 to 6 servings.

Cut leftover meatloaf into thick slices, wrap individually and freeze for hearty meatloaf sandwiches later on a few moments' notice.

A Cozy Christmas Dinner

Gram's Scalloped Potatoes

Sandy Coffey
Cincinnati, OH

A great side for meatloaf dinner or ham that's loved by all the family. Easy too...you don't even peel the potatoes.

2 c. warm water
1 t. cream of tartar
10 to 12 potatoes, sliced
1 onion, chopped and divided
1/2 c. all-purpose flour
2 t. salt, divided

1/2 t. pepper, divided
1/4 c. butter, sliced and divided
10-3/4 oz. can mushroom soup
10-3/4 oz. celery soup
1 c. shredded Cheddar cheese

Mix warm water with cream of tartar in a large bowl. Add potatoes and toss gently; drain. Add half of the potatoes to a greased slow cooker; sprinkle with half each of the onion, flour, salt and pepper. Repeat layering; top with butter and soups. Cover and cook on high setting for 3 hours, until potatoes are nearly tender. Top with cheese; cover and cook on high setting for an additional 30 minutes. Serves 6 to 8.

If your family gift list keeps growing, maybe it's time for a unique gift swap! Have each person draw one name and spend a set amount like $10 on gifts that begin with the recipient's initial...for Barbara, bath beads, a book or bracelet or Tommy, a train, truck or T-shirt. Be sure to open gifts at a family get-together...what fun!

Swiss Steak & Rice

Marie King
Independence, MO

This is a recipe of my mom's that my husband and I love! It's delicious served with homemade biscuits or crescent rolls.

2-lb. beef eye of round roast
2 14-1/2 oz. cans diced
   tomatoes
1 onion, diced
5-1/2 c. water, divided

1/2 c. sugar
1 to 2 t. salt
2 to 3 t. pepper
2 c. long-cooking rice, uncooked

Place roast in a slow cooker. Top with undrained tomatoes, onion, 3-1/2 cups water, sugar, salt and pepper; stir gently. Cover and cook on low setting for 8 to 10 hours. About 30 minutes before roast is done, measure out 2 cups of liquid from slow cooker into a saucepan. Add remaining water and uncooked rice to saucepan; bring to a boil over medium heat. Cover and simmer for 10 to 15 minutes, until rice is tender and most of the liquid is absorbed. Shred roast; serve with rice, topped with extra cooking liquid from slow cooker. Serves 4 to 6.

Don't have a mantel for hanging up stockings? Mount wooden pegs on a board, one for each member of the family. The rest of the year, it'll be a handy place for hanging jackets and sweaters.

A Cozy Christmas Dinner

Bavarian Beef

Kristin Stone
Little Elm, TX

I have a friend who lived in Germany for a few years, and I always enjoy sampling her German cooking. She shared this recipe with me. Although I've modified it a bit to suit my family's tastes, the flavor still brings memories of our fun times crafting together.

2 lbs. beef chuck roast,
    cut into 1-inch cubes
1/2 onion, sliced
1 t. garlic, minced
2 T. oil
3 c. beef broth
2 t. dill seed
2 t. paprika
1 t. caraway seed
1 t. salt
1/4 t. pepper
1/4 c. cold water
3 T. all-purpose flour
cooked spaetzle or thin
    egg noodles
Garnish: sour cream

In a large skillet over medium heat, brown beef, onion and garlic in oil. Drain; place in a large slow cooker. Add broth and seasonings. Cover and cook on high setting for 4 to 5 hours, until beef is tender. Shortly before serving time, combine water and flour in a small bowl. Stir until smooth; gradually stir into beef mixture in slow cooker. Cook and stir for 2 minutes, until thickened. Serve beef and gravy over spaetzle or noodles with a dollop of sour cream on top. Serves 6.

When vacationing throughout the year, look for Christmas ornaments for the tree. Come December, they're sure to bring great memories of family travels and fun!

Make-Ahead Chipotle Burritos

Lorrie Coop
Munday, TX

I love to keep a bag of this hearty chicken mixture on hand in my freezer...it's a real time-saver for busy days! It is so easy to prepare and budget-friendly too.

2 lbs. boneless, skinless chicken breasts
2 15-1/2 oz. cans black beans, drained and rinsed
2 11-oz. cans corn, drained
20-oz. jar salsa
1 canned chipotle pepper in adobo sauce, chopped

2 t. chili powder
2 t. ground cumin
2 t. dried oregano
1 T. salt
flour or corn tortillas
Garnish: sour cream, sliced avocado, shredded Cheddar cheese

Divide chicken between 2 one-gallon plastic zipping freezer bags; set aside. In a large bowl, combine all ingredients except tortillas and garnish; divide between bags. Seal and flatten bags; freeze. To prepare, thaw one bag in refrigerator for 24 hours; place contents of bag in a slow cooker. Cover and cook on low setting for 8 hours, until chicken is very tender. Remove chicken and shred using 2 forks. Return chicken to slow cooker; stir to mix. Serve chicken mixture on tortillas, garnished as desired. Serves 6.

Gifts of time and love are surely the basic ingredients
of a truly merry Christmas.

– Peg Bracken

A Cozy Christmas Dinner

Smothered Beef Tips

Nan Scarborough
Nacogdoches, TX

This makes a wonderful thick warm gravy. When my kids were young, they loved it. During the holidays, we would fill our bowls and sit next to the living room fireplace with all the Christmas lights on and laugh and talk!

2 lbs. beef tips or
    stew beef cubes
salt and pepper to taste
10-3/4 oz. can cream of
    mushroom soup

1/2 c. onion, chopped
11-oz. can corn
3 potatoes, peeled and cubed
2 T. Worcestershire sauce

Place beef in a slow cooker; sprinkle lightly with salt and pepper. Top beef with potatoes; season again with salt and pepper. Spoon soup over potatoes; place onion and undrained corn on top. Sprinkle with Worcestershire sauce. Cover and cook on high setting for 4 hours. To serve, spoon out into bowls. Serves 4 to 6.

Coffee Roast Beef

Debra Oliver
Plainview, TX

This recipe will give you fabulous gravy! You can use a cheaper cut of beef and it will be so tender you won't believe it.

3-lb. beef chuck roast
1.35-oz. pkg. onion soup mix
10-3/4 oz. can cream of
    mushroom soup

2 c. brewed coffee
2 t. cornstarch
2 t. water

Place roast in a slow cooker. Sprinkle with soup mix; spread soup on top and pour coffee over soup. Cover and cook on high setting for 6 to 8 hours, until roast is tender. Remove roast to a serving platter; cover to keep warm. In a cup, dissolve cornstarch in water; add to liquid in slow cooker. Cover and cook for 15 minutes, or until thickened. Serve roast with gravy. Serves 4 to 6.

Easy Kielbasa Supper

Victoria Landry
Shirley, MA

*This recipe brings my Polish heritage to my family
in a tasty way. Serve with fresh rye bread.*

1 yellow onion, sliced
32-oz. jar sauerkraut, drained
  and rinsed
4 to 5 whole peppercorns

Optional: 1 t. caraway seed
4 to 5 potatoes, quartered
1-lb. Kielbasa pork sausage
  sausage

In a slow cooker, layer onion slices and sauerkraut; sprinkle with peppercorns and caraway seed, if using. Add potatoes; place sausage link on top. Cover and cook on high setting for 4 hours. Remove sausage link from crock and slice to serve; stir remaining vegetables to mix. Makes 5 to 6 servings.

Pine cone fire starters are fun to use in the fireplace, or fill a small pail
with them for a special gift. Carefully melt old candle ends or paraffin
in a double boiler and use tongs to dip pine cones. Sprinkle with
a little glitter, if you like, and set on wax paper to dry.

A Cozy Christmas Dinner

Mamma Char's Cabbage Rolls

LaDeana Cooper
Batavia, OH

A wonderful warm-you-up, fill-the-tummy, feel-good meal. My husband requests it quite often during those long winter months.

1 head cabbage, cored
2 lbs. ground beef
1 c. instant rice, uncooked
2 eggs
2 t. garlic powder

3 t. salt, divided
2 t. pepper
3 6-oz. cans tomato paste
4 c. water
1 T. ground thyme

Place cabbage in a microwave-safe bowl. Microwave on high setting for 7 to 8 minutes. Rinse under cold running water until cool enough to handle. Remove 8 to 10 leaves; set aside. Finely shred remaining cabbage and place in the bottom of a large slow cooker. In a large bowl, combine uncooked beef, uncooked rice, eggs, garlic powder, one teaspoon salt and pepper; mix well. Divide beef mixture among cabbage leaves. Roll up leaves, folding in sides and then rolling up burrito-style. Arrange cabbage rolls in slow cooker on top of shredded cabbage. In a separate bowl, mix sauce, water, thyme and remaining salt; ladle over cabbage rolls. Cover and cook on high setting 4 to 5 hours. Makes 6 to 8 servings.

Place newly arrived Christmas cards in a napkin holder, then take a moment at dinnertime to share happy holiday greetings from friends and neighbors.

Cranberry Pork Roast

Terri Scungio
Williamsburg, VA

A friend of mine makes this roast for her annual Christmas Eve dinner. She shared the recipe with me and I tweaked it to our liking. It is definitely a holiday favorite at our house! Serve with mashed potatoes...delicious.

3-lb. boneless rolled pork
   loin roast
14-oz. can whole-berry
   cranberry sauce
1/2 c. brown sugar, packed
1/2 c. cranberry-apple, cranberry
   or apple juice

1 t. dry mustard
1/4 t. ground cloves
1/8 t. nutmeg
2 T. cornstarch
2 T. cold water
salt to taste

Place pork roast in a slow cooker; set aside. In a bowl, stir together cranberry sauce, brown sugar, juice, mustard, cloves and nutmeg; pour over roast. Cover and cook on low setting for 6 to 8 hours, until roast is tender. Remove roast to a serving platter; cover to keep warm. Measure 2 cups of cooking liquid from slow cooker, adding water or more juice to equal 2 cups, if necessary. Pour into a small saucepan; heat over medium heat. In a small bowl, stir together cornstarch and water until a smooth paste forms. Stir into liquid in saucepan; bring to a boil. Cook and stir until thickened. Season sauce with salt; serve with sliced pork. Makes 4 to 6 servings.

Vintage children's toys are always a warm-hearted way to decorate for the holidays. Piled in a wagon, sitting under the Christmas tree or arranged on a mantel, they're sure to bring back special memories.

A Cozy Christmas Dinner

Slow-Cooked Beef Brisket

Annette Ceravolo
Hoover, AL

A family-approved recipe...so good!

5-lb. whole beef brisket,
  trimmed
2 t. garlic, minced
1/2 t. pepper
2 onions, sliced 1/4-inch thick
  and separated into rings
12-oz. bottle chili sauce

2 T. Worcestershire sauce
1-1/2 c. dark ale or beef broth
1 T. brown sugar, packed
Optional: 3 to 4 redskin
  potatoes, quartered
Optional: 1 c. baby carrots

Place brisket fat-side down in a large slow cooker. Spread garlic evenly over brisket; sprinkle with pepper. Arrange onions over brisket; set aside. In a large bowl, combine sauces, ale or broth and brown sugar; pour mixture over brisket and onions. Cover and cook on low setting for 8 hours. Turn brisket over; stir onions into sauce and spoon sauce over brisket. Arrange potatoes and carrots around brisket, if desired. Cover and cook on low setting for an additional one to 2 hours, until brisket and vegetables are tender. Transfer brisket to a cutting board; tent with aluminum foil and let stand for 10 minutes. Stir liquid in slow cooker; spoon off fat and discard. If liquid is too thick, add water, a little at a time, to desired consistency. If too thin, pour into a saucepan; simmer, uncovered, over medium heat until thickened. Thinly slice brisket across the grain. Arrange on a serving platter, surrounded by vegetables, if using. Spoon cooking liquid over brisket before serving. Makes 10 to 12 servings.

Whip up cozy throws in bright-colored fleece...simply snip fringe all around the edges of a two-yard length of fleece. So easy, you can make one for each member of the family in no time at all.

Teriyaki Chicken Thighs

Beth Kramer
Port Saint Lucie, FL

We usually go out for Oriental food on New Year's Eve, but when a blizzard loomed in the weather forecast, I knew we'd be eating at home that night. This recipe was a delicious solution! A chopped salad tossed with gingered dressing completes the meal.

1 onion, cut into thin wedges
20-oz. can pineapple cubes, drained
1 T. oil
8 chicken thighs, skin removed
1/2 t. salt
1/2 to 3/4 c. favorite teriyaki basting and glazing sauce
cooked rice
Garnish: sliced green onions, toasted sesame seed

Place onion and pineapple in a greased 4-quart slow cooker; set aside. Heat oil in a large skillet over medium heat. Add chicken; season with salt. Cook for about 4 minutes per side, until golden. Drain; add chicken to slow cooker. Spoon sauce over chicken. Cover and cook on low setting for 5 hours, or until chicken is no longer pink inside. Serve chicken, onion and pineapple over cooked rice, garnished as desired. Serves 4.

A light and whimsical dessert to serve after a festive meal! Scoop sherbet into stemmed glasses, then slip a fortune cookie over the edge of each glass.

A Cozy Christmas Dinner

Savory Zucchini Bake

JoAnn

I first tried this tasty recipe after harvesting zucchini from my backyard garden. Since zucchini is usually available year 'round, this flavorful side dish can be enjoyed any time.

6 zucchini, sliced 1/2-inch thick
1 t. salt, divided
2 T. olive oil
1 onion, chopped
1 red pepper, chopped
1 clove garlic, minced

1 c. soft bread crumbs
1/3 c. shredded Parmesan
  cheese
1 t. Italian seasoning
1/4 t. pepper
1 T. butter, diced

Place zucchini in a colander; sprinkle with 1/2 teaspoon salt and let stand for 30 minutes. Rinse well; drain and pat dry. Meanwhile, heat oil in a skillet over medium heat. Sauté onion and red pepper until softened, about 5 minutes. Add garlic; cook and stir for one minute. Remove skillet from heat; add zucchini and mix well. In a bowl, mix bread crumbs, cheese, seasoning, remaining salt and pepper. Transfer half of zucchini mixture to a greased 4-quart slow cooker. Sprinkle with half of crumb mixture. Repeat layering; dot with butter. Cover and cook for 4 to 5 hours on low setting, until zucchini is tender. Makes 4 to 6 servings.

Giving a large, hard-to-wrap gift this year? Hide it! Wrap up a smaller gift... for example, a bicycle bell for a new bike or one teeny doll for a doll house. Tie on a gift tag hinting at where to look for the large gift...half the work and twice the fun!

Chicken Gravy for a Crowd

Bekah Brooks
Bluffton, IN

This is an easy, stick-to-your-ribs meal, great for a houseful of teenagers. I love to set the chicken to cook on a weekday while I'm at work, and add the remaining ingredients when I get home. The kids will ask for seconds!

3 26-oz. cans cream of
   mushroom soup
16-oz. container sour cream
6 boneless, skinless chicken
   breasts
4 c. cooked brown rice
3 c. frozen corn, thawed

1 T. onion, minced
1 T. dried parsley
1 t. salt
1/2 t. pepper
mashed potatoes, toasted bread
   or split biscuits

In a large bowl, stir together soup and sour cream. Spread a one-inch layer of soup mixture in the bottom of a large slow cooker. Arrange chicken on top; spoon remaining soup mixture over chicken. Cover and cook on low setting for 6 to 8 hours, until chicken is very tender. Cut up chicken into bite-size pieces; return to slow cooker. Add remaining ingredients except potatoes, toast or biscuits; stir well. Cover and cook for another 30 minutes, or until heated through. To serve, ladle chicken and gravy over mashed potatoes, slices of toast or split biscuits. Serves 15 to 20.

December is jam-packed with baking, shopping and decorating...
take it easy with simple, hearty meals. Make double batches of family
favorites like chili or Sloppy Joes early in the holiday season and
freeze half to heat and eat later. You'll be so glad you did!

A Cozy Christmas Dinner

Un-Cola Pulled Pork

Debi Hodges
Frederica, DE

Tender juicy pork that's oh-so delicious!

1 onion, quartered and halved
2-1/2 to 3-lb. pork shoulder
   or butt roast
1/4 c. cider vinegar
3 T. Worcestershire sauce
2 12-oz. cans lemon-lime soda

2 cloves garlic, minced
1-1/2 t. dry mustard
1/4 t. cayenne pepper
salt and pepper to taste
1 to 2 c. favorite barbecue sauce

Place onion in a slow cooker; top with roast. Sprinkle with vinegar, Worcestershire sauce, soda, garlic and seasonings. Cover and cook on low setting for 7 to 8 hours, or on high setting for 4 to 5 hours, until pork is tender. Remove roast to a large cutting board; shred with 2 forks. Return shredded pork to slow cooker; cover and cook for one additional hour. Drain cooking liquid in slow cooker. Add desired amount of barbecue sauce to pork and onion mixture, little by little. Heat through. Makes 6 to 8 servings.

If guests will be coming & going at different times on Christmas Day, serve a casual buffet instead of a sit-down dinner. With a spread of sliced ham or pulled pork, a choice of breads and sandwich fixin's, warm sides waiting in slow cookers and a luscious dessert tray, guests will happily serve themselves at their own pace.

Herbed Turkey & Wild Rice

Samantha Starks
Madison, WI

I like to stock the freezer with turkey when it's on sale around the holidays. Later, I'll use it for easy and delicious one-pot meals like this. Just add some brown & serve rolls and dinner is ready!

6 slices bacon, coarsely chopped
1 lb. turkey breast tenderloins,
   cut into 3/4-inch cubes
1/2 c. onion, chopped
1/2 c. celery, chopped
1/2 c. carrot, peeled and chopped
10-3/4 oz. cream of chicken
   soup

2 14-oz. cans chicken broth,
   divided
1/4 t. dried thyme
1/8 t. pepper
1-1/4 c. wild rice, uncooked

In a skillet over medium heat, cook bacon until crisp. Stir in turkey; cook until golden, about 3 to 5 minutes. Add vegetables and cook for 2 minutes, stirring occasionally; drain. Meanwhile, add soup and one can broth to a slow cooker; whisk together until smooth. Add remaining broth and seasonings; stir in bacon mixture and uncooked rice. Cover and cook on high setting for 30 minutes. Reduce heat to low setting; cook for 6 to 7 hours, or until rice is tender and liquid is absorbed. Makes 6 servings.

Muffin-tin crayons...a fun snow-day activity for kids! Gather some broken crayons and a mini muffin tin or candy mold that will fit in your slow cooker. Remove wrappers and break crayons into small pieces. Mound up pieces in muffin cups and place tin in slow cooker. Cover and cook on high setting for one to 2 hours, until wax is completely melted. Turn off slow cooker; let stand until wax begins to harden. Transfer to refrigerator and cool for 30 minutes longer.

Sweet
Endings

Gingerbread Pudding Cake

JoAnn

A warm, cozy treat that's out of the ordinary. We like to top it with cinnamon ice cream...scrumptious!

14-1/2 oz. pkg. gingerbread
   cake mix
1/2 c. milk
1/2 c. raisins

2-1/4 c. water
3/4 c. brown sugar, packed
3/4 c. butter, sliced
Optional: vanilla ice cream

In a bowl, combine dry cake mix and milk; stir until moistened. Add raisins; stir until a thick batter forms. Spread batter evenly in the bottom of a lightly greased 4-quart slow cooker; set aside. In a saucepan over medium heat, combine water, brown sugar and butter. Bring to a boil; reduce heat to low. Boil, uncovered, for 2 minutes. Carefully pour brown sugar mixture over batter. Cover and cook on high setting for 2 hours; center will appear moist. Remove crock to a wire rack. Let stand, uncovered, for 45 minutes before serving; center will set up as it cools. To serve, spoon warm cake into bowls. If desired, serve topped with a scoop of ice cream. Makes 8 servings.

Keep all of your family's favorite holiday storybooks in a basket by a cozy chair.
Set aside one night as family night to read your favorites together.

Sweet Endings

Holiday Cranberry Pudding

Susan Schmirler
Hartland, WI

This cherished recipe is eagerly awaited in our family at Christmas and has been passed down through three generations for over 50 years. It's delicious! I often double the recipe as it keeps well in the refrigerator. For holiday convenience the pudding may be prepared days ahead of time...just warm and serve.

2 t. baking soda
1/3 c. boiling water
1 c. fresh cranberries, halved
2 T. sugar

1/4 t. salt
1-1/2 c. all-purpose flour
1/2 c. hot water

In a cup, dissolve baking soda in boiling water. In a bowl, combine cranberries, sugar, salt, baking soda mixture and flour; stir until blended. Pour batter into a well greased 9"x5" loaf pan or a 4-cup pudding mold; cover with aluminum foil. Place pan in a slow cooker; pour hot water around pan. Cover and cook on high setting for 3 to 4 hours, until pudding tests done with a toothpick. Remove pan from crock to a wire rack; uncover and let stand 5 minutes before turning out of pan. Serve slices of warm pudding drizzled with warm Butter Sauce. Serves 6.

Butter Sauce:

1/2 c. butter
1/2 c. whipping cream

1 c. sugar

Melt butter in a saucepan over medium-low heat. Stir in cream and sugar; bring to a boil. Cook, stirring constantly, until sugar is dissolved.

Save those wish lists from little ones each year...a special gift for when they're all grown up.

Apples & Cinnamon Bread Pudding

Cindy Neel
Gooseberry Patch

I always have a few apples left at Christmas from our annual fall trip to the apple orchard. This is a wonderful, comforting way to use them.

2 T. butter, melted
3/4 c. brown sugar, divided
1-1/2 t. cinnamon, divided
2 Gala apples, peeled, cored
   and cubed
2 eggs

12-oz. can evaporated milk
3/4 c. apple juice
2-1/2 c. French bread, torn into
   1-inch pieces
3/4 c. hot water
Garnish: vanilla ice cream

Spread butter in the bottom of a 2-quart casserole dish; sprinkle with 2 tablespoons brown sugar and 1/2 teaspoon cinnamon. Arrange apples in dish; set aside. In a bowl, whisk together eggs, evaporated milk, apple juice and remaining brown sugar and cinnamon. Add bread; toss well until moistened and spoon into dish. Set dish on a trivet in a slow cooker; carefully pour hot water around dish. Cover and cook on high setting for 2-1/2 hours, or until a knife tip inserted in the center tests clean. Serve warm, topped with a scoop of ice cream. Serves 4 to 6.

For delicious apple desserts, some of the best apple varieties are
Granny Smith, Gala and Jonathan as well as old-timers like Rome Beauty,
Northern Spy and Winesap.

Sweet Endings

Mom's Baked Apples

Melody Taynor
Everett, WA

A comforting chilly-weather dessert or a luscious side for roast pork.

4 Granny Smith apples
1/4 c. brown sugar, packed
1/2 t. cinnamon
1/3 c. golden raisins

Optional: 1/3 c. chopped walnuts
1 T. butter, diced
1/2 c. apple juice

Partially core apples from the top; set aside. In a small bowl, mix brown sugar, cinnamon, raisins and walnuts, if using; spoon mixture into apples. Place apples right-side up in a slow cooker; dot with butter. Pour apple juice around apples. Cover and cook on low setting for 5 hours, or on high setting for 2-1/2 hours, until apples are tender. With a large spoon, transfer apples to small bowls. Top with some of the juice mixture over apples; serve warm. Makes 4 servings.

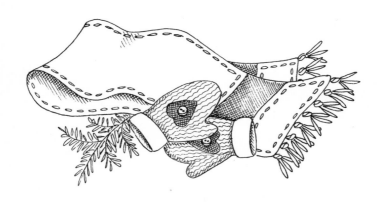

Lots of family members to buy for? Choose a single item like woolly knitted scarves or cozy winter slippers to buy for everyone, in different colors and textures.

Jessica's Mixed Fruit Crisp

Jessica Shrout
Flintstone, MD

This is a wonderful dessert for family gatherings and potlucks. Everyone loves it, and it makes the whole house smell yummy!

1 c. brown sugar, packed
1/2 c. sugar
4 Granny Smith apples, cored
　and cubed
2 Bosc pears, cored and cubed

1/3 c. raisins
2 t. cinnamon
1/4 t. salt
Garnish: vanilla ice cream
　or whipped cream

Mix sugars in a slow cooker, spreading out into an even layer. Top with apples, pears and raisins; sprinkle with cinnamon and salt. Spread Crisp Topping over all. Cover and cook on high setting for 2-1/2 hours. Turn off slow cooker; let stand, covered, for one hour before serving. Scoop crisp into dessert dishes; serve topped with ice cream or whipped cream. Makes 6 to 8 servings.

Crisp Topping:

1 c. long-cooking oats,
　uncooked
1 c. brown sugar, packed
1/4 c. all-purpose flour

1/2 t. cinnamon
1/2 t. nutmeg
3 to 4 T. butter, cubed and
　softened

Mix all ingredients except butter in a bowl. Work in butter with a fork until mixture has a sandy texture.

Take along a slow-cooker dessert to a party or meeting...simply wrap the pot in a towel to insulate it. Serve within an hour or plug it in on a low setting.

Sweet Endings

Saucy Maple Pears

Claire Bertram
Lexington, KY

A friend from Wisconsin brought me a gift bottle of pure maple syrup. I've been looking for special ways to use it... this recipe certainly qualifies!

6 Bosc or Anjou pears, peeled
1/2 c. brown sugar, packed, packed
1/3 c. maple syrup
1 T. butter, melted

1 t. orange zest
1/8 t. ground ginger
1 T. cornstarch
2 T. orange juice

Core pears from the bottom, leaving stems attached; place pears right-side up in a slow cooker. In a bowl, mix brown sugar, syrup, butter, zest and ginger; spoon over pears. Cover and cook on high setting for 2 to 2-1/2 hours, until pears are tender. With a large spoon, remove pears to dessert bowls; cover to keep warm. In a cup, stir cornstarch into orange juice; stir into juices in slow cooker. Cover and cook on high setting for about 10 minutes, until thickened. Spoon sauce over pears. Serves 6.

Oh, heart, let's never grow too old
To smile anew, when Christmas comes,
At tassels red and tinsel thread,
And tarlatan bags of sugarplums.

– Nancy Byrd Turner

Festive Pumpkin Bread Pudding

Donna Reid
Payson, AZ

My family loves this bread pudding during autumn and into the Christmas season. I use pumpkins from my garden to make pumpkin purée and the flavor is amazing!

3 eggs
1-1/2 c. milk
1 c. canned pumpkin
3/4 c. brown sugar, packed
2 t. vanilla extract
1 t. cinnamon
1/2 t. nutmeg
1/4 t. ground cloves

1/2 t. salt
1 loaf brioche bread, cut into
   1-inch cubes
1/2 c. golden raisins
1 T. butter
Garnish: whipped cream or
   vanilla ice cream

In a bowl, combine eggs, milk, pumpkin, brown sugar, vanilla, spices and salt. Whisk until smooth; set aside. In a separate bowl, toss bread cubes with raisins. Spread butter inside a slow cooker; transfer bread mixture to slow cooker. Pour milk mixture evenly over bread mixture, pressing down so bread will soak up the liquid. Cover and cook on high setting for 2 to 2-1/2 hours, until set and top is golden and puffy. Serve warm or at room temperature, garnished with whipped cream or vanilla ice cream. Serves 6.

Fresh whipped cream makes any dessert even more delectable. It's easy too. Combine one cup whipping cream with 1/4 cup powdered sugar and one teaspoon vanilla extract in a chilled bowl. Beat with chilled beaters until stiff peaks form.

Sweet Endings

Gingered Apple-Raisin Compote

Vickie

Simple to make ahead...just warm again shortly before serving.

6 Gala apples, peeled, cored
   and sliced
1 c. brown sugar, packed
1 c. raisins
1/3 c. chopped walnuts, toasted
1/2 c. water

2-inch piece fresh ginger, peeled
   and minced
zest and juice of 1 lemon
4 4-inch cinnamon sticks
Optional: crushed gingersnap
   cookies

Combine all ingredients except cinnamon sticks and gingersnaps in a slow cooker. Stir gently; tuck in cinnamon sticks. Cover and cook on low setting for 5 hours, or on high setting for 3 hours. Stir; discard cinnamon sticks. Serve warm, topped with gingersnap crumbs, if desired. Makes 6 servings.

Mini slow cookers are terrific for melting chocolate with no burning or scorching! Fill up the crock with chips or chunks of chocolate and cook on low setting until melted. Stir, then dip in cookies, pretzels and pieces of fruit, or drizzle over desserts of all kinds. Yum!

Delectable Lemon Cheesecake

Cheri Maxwell
Gulf Breeze, FL

With all the delicious excesses of holiday meals and occasions, a light-tasting dessert is very welcome! I like to serve slices of this cheesecake garnished with a puff of whipped cream and a twist of lemon peel.

1 c. vanilla wafers, crumbled
3 T. butter, melted
2/3 c. plus 1 T. sugar, divided
1-1/2 t. lemon zest, divided
2 8-oz. pkgs. cream cheese,
    softened

2 eggs
1 T. all-purpose flour
2 T. lemon juice

In a bowl, combine vanilla wafer crumbs, melted butter, one tablespoon sugar and 1/2 teaspoon lemon zest. Pat into a 7" round springform pan; set aside. In a separate bowl, beat together cream cheese and remaining sugar with an electric mixer on medium speed until smooth. Add eggs; beat for 3 minutes. Add flour, lemon juice and remaining lemon zest; continue beating for one minute. Pour filling into crust. Set pan on a trivet in a slow cooker. Cover and cook on high setting for 2-1/2 to 3 hours. Turn off slow cooker; let stand, covered, for one to 2 hours. Remove pan from slow cooker; cool completely before removing sides of pan. Cover and chill until serving time. Serves 8.

Wrapped in love! Use children's drawings as wrapping paper for gifts from the kitchen. Perfect for grandparents and aunts & uncles.

Sweet Endings

Pineapple Nut Loaf

Zoe Bennett
Columbia, SC

When I was growing up, I loved to give little tea parties for my dolls. Mom would bake this sweet, tender bread for me to serve with cream cheese...so dainty! Now I bake it for my own little girl.

2-3/4 c. all-purpose flour	1 c. chopped dates
3/4 c. sugar	1 c. chopped walnuts
1 T. baking powder	1 egg, beaten
3/4 t. salt	1/3 c. milk
1 c. crushed pineapple, drained	1/3 c. butter, melted

In a bowl, mix together flour, sugar, baking powder and salt. In a separate bowl, combine remaining ingredients. Add pineapple mixture to flour mixture; stir until moistened. Pour into a well greased and floured 32-ounce metal coffee can; cover with aluminum foil. Place in a slow cooker. Cover and cook on high setting for 3 to 4 hours, until loaf tests done with a toothpick inserted in the center. Remove can to a wire rack; uncover and let stand for 5 minutes. Turn out loaf onto wire rack; cool. Makes one loaf.

Give your home a spicy holiday scent year 'round. Cover oranges with whole cloves, piercing the peels in swirly designs or simply covering the fruit at random. Roll in cinnamon and ginger, then stack in a wooden bowl. Once dried, the oranges will remain fragrant for months.

Rocky Road Chocolate Cake

Linda Behling
Cecil, PA

If you are looking for a dessert for that holiday buffet table that really says "chocolate goodness" to you, this is it! It's always the first dessert to disappear at my holiday gatherings. Trying to keep the kids away from it until they have eaten their regular meal is always interesting!

18-1/4 oz. pkg. German
   chocolate cake mix
3.9-oz. pkg. instant chocolate
   pudding mix
3 eggs, lightly beaten
8-oz. container sour cream
1/3 c. butter, melted
1 t. vanilla extract

3-1/4 c. milk, divided
3.4-oz. pkg. cook & serve
   chocolate pudding mix
1-1/2 c. mini marshmallows
6-oz. pkg. semi-sweet chocolate
   chips
1/2 c. chopped pecans, toasted
Optional: vanilla ice cream

In a bowl, combine dry cake mix, dry instant pudding mix, eggs, sour cream, melted butter, vanilla and 1-1/4 cups milk. Beat with an electric mixer on medium speed for 2 minutes. Pour batter into a lightly greased 4-quart slow cooker. Sprinkle dry cook & serve pudding mix over batter. In a heavy saucepan over medium heat, heat remaining milk, stirring often, for 3 to 5 minutes; do not boil. Slowly pour hot milk over pudding. Cover and cook on low setting for 3-1/2 hours; turn off slow cooker. Cake will set up as it stands. Uncover; sprinkle cake with remaining ingredients. Let stand for 15 minutes, or until marshmallows are slightly melted. Spoon into dessert dishes, topped with ice cream, if desired. Serves 8 to 10.

Add a welcoming row of twinkling luminarias along the front walk and your house will be party perfect!

Sweet Endings

Rich Chocolate Pots

Emma Jacobs
Idaho Falls, ID

*Small servings of this luscious chocolate pudding are perfect
on buffets for "just a taste" of something sweet.*

6 eggs
1 qt. whipping cream
1/2 t. salt
2-2/3 c. semi-sweet chocolate
    chips

Garnish: whipped cream
Optional: chocolate curls

In a slow cooker, whisk together eggs, cream and salt; stir in chocolate chips. Cover and cook on high setting for 30 minutes, until chocolate chips have melted; whisk until smooth. Turn to low setting. Cover and cook for another 30 minutes; whisk. Cover and continue cooking on low setting for about 1-1/4 hours, until edges are set. Just before serving, whisk again; spoon into small dessert bowls. Top with whipped cream; garnish with chocolate curls, if desired. Serves 8 to 10.

Slip a packet of spiced tea into a Christmas card to a dear friend...
she can enjoy a hot cup of tea while reading your latest news.

Spicy Peaches with Raspberry Sauce

Louise Greer
Cartersville, GA

Your house will smell so Christmasy and inviting with this simply yet incredibly good dessert simmering away!

2 29-oz. cans peach halves
   in syrup
cinnamon, nutmeg and ground
   cloves to taste
2 c. light brown sugar, packed
2 T. butter, diced

1 T. vanilla extract
Optional: raisins, prunes,
   figs or dates
Garnish: vanilla ice cream,
   warmed raspberry sauce

Combine undrained peaches and remaining ingredients except garnish in a slow cooker; stir gently to mix. Cover and cook on high setting for 2 hours, until peaches are glazed and tender. To serve, place a scoop of ice cream in each bowl; top with 2 peach halves and and a generous serving of raspberry sauce. Serves 12.

Tuck in the kids with visions of sugarplums...stitch up some
simple pillowcases from holiday fabric.

Sweet Endings

Razzleberry Crisp

Kay Marone
Des Moines, IA

My mother made this yummy fruit crisp year 'round with different flavors of fruit pie filling and we kids loved it. At Christmastime, no matter what kind of fruit she used, we would call it razzleberry, thinking of the old Mr. Magoo's Christmas Carol cartoon.

21-oz. can raspberry or other
    fruit pie filling
1/2 c. quick-cooking oats,
    uncooked
2/3 c. brown sugar, packed

1/2 c. all-purpose flour
1 t. brown sugar, packed
1/3 c. butter, softened
Optional: half-and-half

Place pie filling in a lightly greased slow cooker; set aside. In a bowl, combine remaining ingredients except butter; cut in butter with a fork until crumbly. Sprinkle oat mixture over pie filling. Cover and cook on low setting for 4 to 5 hours, until hot and bubbly. Serve warm, drizzled with half-and-half, if desired. Serves 4.

As winter approaches, host a dessert get-together with friends and ask each to bring a gently-worn winter coat or pair of new mittens. Donate them to a local shelter...kindness that will warm the chilly days ahead.

Old-Fashioned Rice Pudding

Janice Mullins
Kingston, TN

A down-home dessert that's very comforting on a cold day. It's delicious served warm or cold...so easy, just mix it & forget it! For the holidays I'll sometimes use dried cranberries instead of raisins.

2-1/2 c. cooked rice
12-oz. can evaporated milk
3 eggs, beaten
2/3 c. brown sugar, packed

3 T. butter, softened
2 t. vanilla extract
1 t. nutmeg
1 c. raisins

Combine all ingredients in a bowl; mix gently. Spoon into a lightly greased slow cooker. Cover and cook on low setting for 5 hours. Serve warm or chilled. Makes 4 to 6 servings.

Gather everyone for a fireside meal...so cozy on a snowy day! Cook hot dogs on long forks or use pie irons to make pocket pies. You can even roast foil-wrapped potatoes in the coals. Let the kids make s'mores for a sweet ending.

Sweet Endings

Pumpkin Pie Pudding

Janis Parr
Campbellford, Ontario

*Our family loves anything pumpkin-flavored and this dessert
is a very big hit, especially at Christmas.*

15-oz. can pumpkin
12-oz. can evaporated milk
3/4 c. sugar
1/2 c. biscuit baking mix
2 eggs, beaten

2-1/2 T. butter, melted
1 T. pumpkin pie spice
2-1/2 t. vanilla extract
Garnish: whipped cream

Mix together all ingredients except garnish in a bowl. Spoon into a
slow cooker. Cover and cook on low setting for 7 hours. Serve warm,
topped with whipped cream. Makes 4 to 6 servings.

A sweet centerpiece...place a plump pillar candle
on a clear glass dish and surround it
with peppermint candies.

Rich Bread Pudding

Diana Chaney
Olathe, KS

We save odds & ends of bread, cinnamon rolls, crescents and what-have-you throughout the holiday season, filling a bag in the freezer. When we have enough bread cubes, we know it's time to make the pudding. Thriftiness never tasted so good!

5 eggs, beaten
3/4 c. brown sugar, packed
3-1/2 c. milk
2 T. cinnamon
2 t. vanilla extract
1/2 t. salt

1 T. butter, melted
6 c. bread or rolls, cubed
Optional: 1/2 c. golden raisins
Garnish: vanilla ice cream,
    whipped cream or
    half-and-half

Combine all ingredients except garnish in a large bowl. Mix together until smooth and bread crumbs are well moistened. Transfer to a greased slow cooker. Cover and cook on high setting for 3-1/2 hours, or until a knife tip stuck in the center tests nearly clean. Lift lid and set slightly off-center, to allow excess moisture to escape; continue cooking for 30 minutes. Serve warm, garnished as desired. Serves 6 to 8.

Take a holiday photo of your family in the same place, same position each year, for example in the front of the Christmas tree... a sweet record of how the kids have grown!

Sweet Endings

Homemade Caramel Sauce

Gretchen Hickman
Galva, IL

This sauce is delicious! My great-aunt owned an apple orchard for many years, so she really knew her apple desserts. Serve this sauce for dipping apples or drizzle it over sliced apples and apple desserts.

14-oz. can sweetened
   condensed milk
1/2 c. butter, sliced

2 c. brown sugar, packed
3/4 c. light corn syrup
1/8 t. salt

Combine all ingredients in a heavy saucepan over medium heat. Bring to a boil, stirring constantly. Cover and cook for about 5 minutes, until mixture reaches the soft-ball stage, or 234 to 243 degrees on a candy thermometer. Transfer into a mini slow cooker on low setting for serving. Cover and refrigerate any leftovers. Makes about 2 cups.

Need a gift for a special family? Give a board game or a couple of card games along with a tin filled with homemade goodies... it'll be much appreciated on the next snow day!

Triple Chocolate Gooey Cake

Carol Lytle
Columbus, OH

The easiest-ever way to serve up a tummy-warming chocolatey dessert for a crowd!

2 9-oz. pkgs. chocolate
    cake mix
3.9-oz. pkg. instant chocolate
    pudding mix
16-oz. container sour cream
4 eggs, beaten

3/4 c. oil
1 c. water
6-oz. pkg. semi-sweet chocolate
    chips
Garnish: vanilla ice cream

In a large bowl, combine dry mixes and remaining ingredients except garnish. Mix well; pour into a well greased slow cooker. Cover and cook on low setting for 6 to 8 hours, or on high setting for 3 to 4 hours. Serve warm, scooped into dessert bowls and topped with ice cream. Makes 8 to 10 servings.

Be sure to pick up a pint or two of ice cream in peppermint, cinnamon and other delicious seasonal flavors when they're available. What a special touch for holiday desserts!

Sweet Endings

Butterscotch Fondue

Sherry Gordon
Arlington Heights, IL

In a word, irresistible! This smooth, warm butterscotch makes a wonderful topping for ice cream or cake too.

2 14-oz. cans sweetened
   condensed milk
2 c. brown sugar, packed
1 c. butter, melted
2/3 c. light corn syrup

1 t. vanilla extract
1/4 c. rum or milk
sponge cake or brownie
   cubes, sliced apples, whole
   strawberries, small cookies

In a 4-quart slow cooker, combine condensed milk, brown sugar, butter, corn syrup and vanilla. Cover and cook on low setting for 3 hours. Whisk in rum or milk until smooth. Keep warm on low setting for serving up to 2 hours, stirring occasionally. Serve with desired dippers. Makes about 5 cups.

A trip to the grocery store will yield lots of fun decorations for a gingerbread house...candy-coated chocolates, cinnamon candies, peppermints, cereal shapes and mini pretzels. Join the kids and just use your imagination!

Chocolate-Peanut Butter Drops

Connie Hilty
Pearland, TX

My go-to recipe for Christmas gifts...in no time at all, I have enough nutty chocolate candy for friends, neighbors and co-workers!

10-oz. jar salted dry-roasted
  peanuts
11-1/2 oz. pkg. semi-sweet
  chocolate chips

1/2 c. creamy peanut butter
24-oz. pkg. melting chocolate,
  chopped or broken up

Layer all ingredients in a slow cooker. Cover and cook on high setting for one hour, stirring occasionally, or until chocolate is melted. Stir again until smooth. Drop by tablespoonfuls onto wax paper; let stand until set. Store in an airtight container. Makes about 4 dozen pieces.

For a terrific eggnog punch in a jiffy, combine one quart eggnog,
2 pints softened peppermint ice cream and one cup ginger ale.
Delicious and easy to double for a crowd.

Sweet Endings

Chewy Peanut Candy

Amy Butcher
Columbus, GA

A crockery confection that's a little different from the others...
it tastes like your favorite peanut candy bar!

1/4 c. butter, sliced
3 c. super-fine sugar
1 c. light corn syrup
2 t. vanilla extract

2 t. baking soda
4 c. lightly salted dry-roasted
   peanuts

In a large slow cooker, combine butter, sugar, corn syrup and vanilla. Cover and cook on high setting for one hour. Stir well; add baking soda. Cover and continue cooking for 15 to 30 minutes, until mixture is golden. Add peanuts; stir until well coated. Line 2 baking sheets with parchment paper. Using oven mitts, pour mixture out onto parchment paper-lined baking sheets; spread out with a spatula. Let stand for about one hour, until cool; tear into bite-size pieces. Store in an airtight container, with layers separated by parchment or wax paper. Makes about 3 pounds.

Fill an apothecary jar with old-fashioned ribbon candy...
pretty to look at and sweet to sample!

Chocolate Corn Chip Crunch

Melanie Lowe
Dover, DE

*This crunchy, chocolatey, salty-sweet confection will be
a big hit at your next party, or bagged up for gifts!*

1/2 c. butter, sliced
11-1/2 oz. pkg. semi-sweet
  chocolate chips
1/2 c. brown sugar, packed
Optional: 2 T. creamy peanut
  butter

2 c. corn chips, coarsely crushed
2 c. mini pretzel twists, coarsely
  crushed
Optional: 1/2 c. chopped peanuts

In a large slow cooker, combine butter, chocolate chips, brown sugar
and peanut butter, if using. Cover and cook on high setting for one to
1-1/2 hours, until chocolate is melted; stir well. Add corn chips and
pretzels; stir gently until coated. Using oven mitts, pour mixture out
onto parchment paper-lined baking sheets; spread out with a wooden
spoon. Sprinkle peanuts on top, if using; press lightly. Refrigerate for
about one hour, until set. Break into pieces. Store in an airtight
container. Makes about 7 cups.

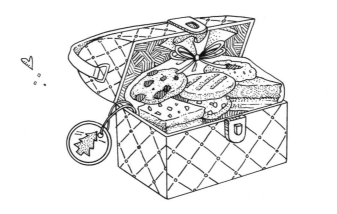

Give a vintage-style lunchbox filled with homemade candy...the lunchbox
makes a great keepsake long after the candy is gone.

Sweet Endings

Triple Chocolate Clusters

Justine Hutchings
New York Mills, NY

The most delicious, easiest candy you ever made!

16-oz. jar salted dry-roasted peanuts
16-oz. jar unsalted dry-roasted peanuts
11-1/2 oz. pkg. semi-sweet chocolate chips

4 1-oz. sqs. sweet baking chocolate, broken up
2 24-oz. pkgs. white melting chocolate, chopped or broken up

In a large slow cooker, layer all ingredients in order listed. Cover and cook on low setting for 3 hours, or until chocolate is soft but not melted. Stir until blended and smooth. Drop by teaspoonfuls onto wax paper-lined baking sheets. Let stand until set. Store in an airtight container. Makes about 12 to 14 dozen pieces.

Get in the holiday spirit by trimming a tabletop tree! Look around the house for items like sparkly clip earrings or tiny toys and dolls to use as ornaments... even clip figures from Christmas cards or make a tiny paper chain. Such fun!

Rocky Road Candy

Lori Rosenberg
University Heights, OH

These gooey chocolate-marshmallow delights couldn't be simpler to prepare and are quick to disappear!

11-1/2 oz. pkg. semi-sweet
   chocolate chips

4 c. mini marshmallows
1-3/4 c. chopped walnuts

Pour chocolate chips into a slow cooker. Cover and cook on high setting for 30 minutes; stir. Continue cooking, checking every 15 minutes, until chocolate is melted. Stir in marshmallows with a large spoon; stir in walnuts. Remove crock from its base. Using 2 spoons, drop candy by teaspoonfuls onto parchment paper-lined baking sheets. Refrigerate until cooled and set. Store in an airtight container. Makes about 11 cups.

Homemade candy is always a welcome gift! Make the gift even sweeter...place individual candies in mini paper muffin cups and arrange in a decorated box.

Sweet Endings

Christmas Sugared Walnuts

Gladys Kielar
Whitehouse, OH

Sugar and spice and everything nice! We make these treats every year to share with family & friends.

1 lb. walnut halves
1/2 c. butter, melted
1/2 c. powdered sugar
1-1/2 t. cinnamon

1/4 t. allspice
1/4 t. ground ginger
1/8 t. ground cloves

In a slow cooker, stir together walnuts and butter until combined. Add powdered sugar, stirring to coat walnuts evenly. Cover and cook on high setting for 15 minutes. Turn heat to low setting. Cook, uncovered, for about 2 hours, stirring occasionally, until nuts are coated with a crisp glaze. Transfer nuts to a serving bowl. Combine spices in a cup. Sprinkle spice mixture over nuts, stirring to coat evenly. Cool completely on parchment paper-lined baking sheets. Store in an airtight container. Makes 3 to 4 cups.

Make crinkled gift bag filler in a jiffy with a paper shredder. Simply run odds & ends of leftover wrapping paper through the shredder... ready to nestle in baskets and gift bags!

Cinnamon-Sugar Almonds

Marian Buckley
Fontana, CA

Fill clear plastic icing cones with these terrific nuts and tie with a bow for perfect take-home gifts.

1-1/2 c. sugar
3 T. cinnamon
1/8 t. salt

1 egg white
1-1/2 t. vanilla extract
3 c. whole almonds

In a small bowl, mix together sugar, cinnamon and salt; set aside. In a large bowl, whisk together egg white and vanilla until frothy. Add almonds to egg mixture; toss to coat thoroughly. Sprinkle with sugar mixture; toss again to coat well. Add almonds to a slow cooker generously coated with non-stick vegetable spray. Cover and cook on high setting for 2 hours, stirring every 20 minutes. Spread out almonds on parchment paper-lined baking sheets; cool completely. Store in an airtight container. Makes about 3 cups.

Blessed with lots of co-workers to share the holiday spirit with? Surprise each of them with a clear plastic cup, filled with homemade treats and wrapped in shiny cellophane...cheers!

Sweet Endings

Sweet & Salty Pretzel Mix

Laura Fuller
Fort Wayne, IN

Deliciously crunchable! I like to attach a festively ribboned package of this homemade snack to a favorite movie DVD for gift-giving.

16-oz. pkg. pretzel sticks, broken
4 c. bite-size crispy corn cereal squares
4 c. salted cashews
1 c. butter, sliced
1 c. powdered sugar
1/2 c. brown sugar, packed
2 t. cinnamon

Combine pretzels, cereal and cashews in a large slow cooker; set aside. Melt butter in a saucepan over medium-low heat. Stir in sugars and cinnamon; stir until well blended. Drizzle sugar mixture over pretzel mixture. Cook, uncovered, on high setting for 2 to 3 hours, until mixture is glazed. Spread mixture on parchment paper-lined baking sheets; cool completely. Store in an airtight container. Makes about 16 cups.

A holiday gift just in time...give a New Year's basket filled with party hats, festive noisemakers, glittery confetti and plenty of treats too!

Cherry Chocolate Heaven

Deidre Cartmill
Broken Arrow, OK

*My co-workers love it when I take this to potlucks at work
on a cold winter day!*

21-oz. can cherry pie filling
18-1/2 oz. pkg. chocolate
   cake mix

1/2 c. butter
Garnish: vanilla ice cream

Spoon pie filling into a greased slow cooker; set aside. In a bowl, use
a fork to stir dry cake mix and butter until slightly crumbly. Spread
mixture over pie filling. Cover and cook on low setting for 3 to 4 hours,
or on high setting for 2 hours. Serve warm, topped with ice cream.
Makes 10 to 12 servings.

A hug is the perfect gift — one size fits all,
and nobody minds if you exchange it.

— Ivern Ball

Sweet Endings

Pineapple Upside-Down Cake

Marian Buckley
Fontana, CA

A warm and comforting cake that's delicious year 'round.

1 c. brown sugar, packed
1/4 c. butter, melted
20-oz. can pineapple rings,
   drained and juice reserved
10 maraschino cherries, drained
   and stems removed

15-1/4 oz. pkg. yellow cake mix
1/2 c. oil
3 eggs, beaten

In a small bowl, mix brown sugar and melted butter. Spread evenly in the bottom of a greased 6-quart slow cooker. Arrange pineapple rings over brown sugar mixture in a single layer, cutting as needed to fit. Place a cherry in center of each pineapple ring; place any leftover cherries around pineapple rings and set aside. Combine pineapple juice with enough water to equal one cup. Prepare cake mix with oil and eggs according to package directions, using juice mixture instead of water called for. Pour batter over pineapple and cherries. Cover and cook on high setting for 2-1/2 to 3 hours, until a toothpick inserted in the center tests clean. Remove crock to a wire rack; uncover and allow to cool for 15 minutes. Top crock with a serving plate; carefully turn cake out onto plate. Makes 10 to 12 servings.

When visiting friends during the holidays, slip an ornament onto their tree with a small gift tag...when they take down the tree, it'll be a thoughtful after-Christmas surprise!

Index

Index

Index

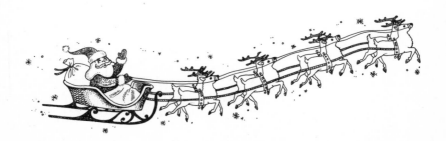